T0208331

UNCERTAINTY OF COMMUNICATION: INTERPRETING GLOBAL SOCIAL MEDIA COMMUNICATION IN A WAY OF PHILOSOPHY OF SCIENCE

DONG CHAO

authorHOUSE®

AuthorHouse™
1663 Liberty Drive
Bloomington, IN 47403
www.authorhouse.com
Phone: 833-262-8899

Published by AuthorHouse 05/07/2021

ISBN: 978-1-6655-2523-7 (sc)
ISBN: 978-1-6655-2521-3 (hc)
ISBN: 978-1-6655-2522-0 (e)

Library of Congress Control Number: 2021909625

CONTENTS

ABSTRACT

Innis believes that every civilization has a biased medium. Nowadays, centralized media organizations are offset by decentralized media forms, but they still keep unity in this diverse media environment. The main performance is that, as professional social organizations, media are impacted and replaced by social media on platforms. It can be said that, in terms of media popularity, current "social media" are becoming what Innis called "biased" media. Social media are affecting every aspect of communication in contemporary society. However, our research on social media is relatively lagging behind its development. As a practice-oriented discipline practice with the history of interdisciplinary research, many sociological concepts are introduced to the communication field to explain the development of social media, such as "self-organization theory", "empowerment theory", "field theory", "high-dimensional media", etc. Though these concepts help to narrow the gap between the theoretical research and the practice to some extent, it has not formed a complete interpretation system for communication study to explain the everchanging media environment.

Therefore, this paper attempts to jump out of the original interpretation framework of social science and to explain new communication phenomena in a novel way of philosophy of science. The paper believes that the development of the communication revolution, especially the recent information technology revolution, not only makes human being step into an advanced information society but also fundamentally changes the traditional communication methods. So, when traditional communication science is insufficient to interpret novel media phenomena, using the philosophy of science to explain these new communication phenomena is not only feasible but also necessary. This paper thinks that the so-called philosophy of science is the product of "transforming science knowledge into wisdom", including not only the concept and methodology of natural science, but also the humanistic understanding of modern science.

The paper first defines the concept of philosophy of science and social media, then studies the new communication features on social media under the influence of technological changes, including the emergence and change of communication factors such as content, channel, audience, relationship, emotion, and scenario, summarizes the relationship between the speed and dimension change of communication and technological revolution. Based on that, this paper redefines the concept of "information", and explains the six new communication features with the concepts in the philosophy of science, including the "information entropy", "uncertainty", "many worlds", "probability" and "quantum correlation". Besides, this paper starts with the basic unit of social media, gradually establishes an interpretation framework for social media, re-explaining its information, effect, ontological structure, function, and the whole system. Also, the research establishes a hypothetic efficiency equation for interpreting social media. At last, this paper verifies the proposed framework by three different case studies, "British Death Van" in 2019, "yellow vests movement" and NBA commissioner's controversial speech.

There are certainly still a number of flaws in this study, including the systematicness of the applied theories, the systematicness of new communication knowledge, the type description of research objects, and the appropriateness of core theories, which all need to be improved and strengthened.

PREFACE

Since the new century, social media has developed rapidly through the iteration of information technology, and has covered every aspect of our lives, changing not only the lives and values of individuals, but also, to a large extent, the lives and values of society as a whole. People's access to information has moved from a single channel to a variety of choices, from fixed to timely, from one-way communication to instant interaction, and from the text used in paper media to images on the screen, and on the basis of the popularity of 5G and Internet technology, a richer audio-visual experience such as virtual reality has been opened up, which shows that in the world of information dissemination Media content, media forms, and media technologies are evolving round after round. In the world of information dissemination, both the content and the media channels have undergone several revolutions, and the resulting values of individuals and society are also changing in proportion to the acceleration of information dissemination. The understanding of these new communication phenomena requires new explanations that go beyond traditional communication science. It can be said that the original interpretation of communication, whether from the technical, practical, cultural, ideological and other perspectives as well as for the discipline of communication has laid a rich foundation, generations of communication scholars in the past hundred years, research, from the theoretical basis to the practical understanding of communication has made great contributions to communication, the masters of communication, including Albert Cantrell, Anthony Giddens, Antonioni Gramsci, Cooley, Mead, Rogers, Schramm, Marcuse, Baudrillard, McLuhan, Schiller, and many others have all made their contributions. After communication science entered China in the 1980s, a large number of excellent communication scholars emerged in China, such as Ming Anxiang, Fan Dongsheng, Xu Yaokui, Dai Yuanguang, Shao Peiren, Zheng Beiwei, Zhang Lundong, Chen Yunzhao, etc., who played a role in the introduction and promotion of communication science, and the research results of communication science were fruitful. However, communication research needs constant breakthroughs.

As far as the paradigm of communication research is concerned, Wang Yihong, in a survey of 30 years of communication research in China, suggests that "communication must have its own 'spillover' effect and cannot be confined to the shackles of the discipline itself.[1] From the perspective of the currently accepted paradigm, most scholars have looked at communication beyond the functional paradigm and achieved richer results, especially in recent years, the "media science" proposed by the French scholar Debray has become one of the main schools of communication studies in China, and the Danish scholar Stig Schaiva has attributed the past research that relied on effects and content to "The role of the media in society can be said to be the mainstream paradigm in recent years. From a philosophical point of view, the philosophical perspectives that have been put forward to reflect on communication include the philosophy of media technology proposed by German scholar Kittler, the philosophical thinking proposed by scholars of cultural studies in communication, and even the suggestion that "philosophy may ultimately be nothing more than media theory. ......,[2]Among them, it is worth noting that the studies from the perspective of philosophy of science are more enlightening, relatively less researched, and have more room for depth, supplementation and reflection. A cautious and reverent attempt to stand on the research of the predecessors for a new interpretive perspective is also the call of some prominent communication scholars in China, as Xu Yaokui, a researcher at the Academy of Social Sciences, points out in his article, "If we still turn in circles in the box drawn by a few founders of communication, are we too conservative, too backward, too rigid then?"[3]

---

[1] Wang Yihong, An Examination of 30 Years of Historical Stages in the Development of Communication Studies, Journalism and Communication Research,2009, p.10
[2] Graham Harman, Huang Furong, Bells and Whistles,A More Discursive Positivism, Southwest Normal University Press, 2018, p.219
[3] Xu Yaokui, The gains and losses of communication research in China, Journalism and Communication Research, 1998.12

In the face of new communication phenomena and new communication practices, some valuable additions and reflections can be made from the perspective of the philosophy of science. Kuhn, a giant in the philosophy of science, proposed that scientific research is a revolution, a revolution of one scientific discovery over the previous one. From this perspective, this paper argues that traditional communication research has encountered a dilemma, so a new communication interpretation is needed for a disciplinary paradigm revolution to accommodate the development of the discipline. The initial goal of this paper is to add a scientific-philosophical dimension to the new communication phenomenon based on previous research. Negel considers scientific explanation as "the answer to the 'why' question" and "as the scenario changes, different kinds of answers are appropriate to it."[4] It should be noted that this paper is an exploration of a scientific-philosophical explanation of social media, a perspective on social media and even information communication, an objective statement with independent criteria,[5]and, by its nature, a hypothesis of theoretical explanation, like any other explanation or theory.

[4] Ernest Nagel, The Structure of Science, Xu Xiangdong, Shanghai Translation Press, 2005, p. 16
[5] Wang Xiaoyang, Consciousness Studies, Shanghai People's Publishing House, 2019, p. 7

PROBLEM FORMULATION

Since the beginning of communication science, media forms have undergone a revolutionary change from paper-based media to a century of practice, and communication vehicles, modes and practices have been constantly changing. Since online media entered China in 1994, especially in the new century, social media has gradually become the main tool for social information dissemination. On a global level, the widespread use of social media platforms such as Twitter and Facebook has not only contributed to the expression of personal information production, but even to the emergence of self-media in general, and has also profoundly affected all aspects of global politics, culture, and economy. 2011 Occupy Wall Street movement, 2012 and 2016 U.S. presidential elections, the four-year extension of Britain's exit from the European Union, 2018's Some major international events, such as the French Yellow Vest movement, have been profoundly influenced by social media. The media change has turned the world upside down, the social media flood rolls on, and there are constantly new social media emerging, such as Now This, Facebook, Snapchat, Twitter, Instagram, YouTube, Buzzfeed, Clipboard, etc. in foreign countries, and Weibo, WeChat, Headline, Jitterbug, etc. in China, these These media have been integrated with newspapers, radio and TV as the main means of information dissemination in today's society.The emergence of personal applications (APPs) relying on the Internet, especially mobile Internet as a means of communication, has not only revolutionized information dissemination, but also redefined every aspect of people's lives in terms of clothing, food, housing and transportation: YELP, Taobao, Jingdong, Meituan, VW Review, Ctrip, Where to go, Audemars Piguet, Drip and other applications have become an indispensable part of people's lives. At the same time, the structural collection of these life application APPs has profoundly sculpted social life and social culture, and these life application APPs are a new type of social media distinguished from simple news release and information interaction for the purpose. Marxism believes that productivity and relations of production determine the superstructure at the social level, and this assertion still applies in the information communication society, where "information bits" are the means of production in the information society, and the structured use of "information bits" to create value is the productivity. In the current information society, the characteristics of social culture, emotional cognition, and social participation are also typical of "information technology". It can be said that social media has become an important part of profound participation in social change.

Social media is an important part of the development of information dissemination practices. Social media creates and disseminates a wide variety of information events every day, and an ordinary person is overwhelmed by the information created and disseminated by social media every day when he opens his eyes. The growth and widespread use of social media at the practical level has become commonplace in this society. At the level of theoretical explanations of these communication phenomena, there has been a great deal of useful work done in communication studies. Practice and theory are in a complementary relationship, and the dazzling media practices have also pushed to draw from the existing theoretical paradigms in communication to develop a universal explanatory grounded theory. The basic explanatory theories are constantly enriched and changed with the development of social media, especially in the face of the new media forms that are constantly emerging, which can be useful to supplement and enrich the basic theories of communication from multiple perspectives. From the perspective of China's theoretical research, it has been forty years since the introduction of communication studies in the 1980s. Scholars in China are exploring new explanatory theories on the one hand, and calling on the academic community to join in the exploration of new explanations on the other. In his reflection on communication research, Sun Xupei, a communication scholar in China, pointed out that "on the whole, communication research in China is generally catch-up research" [6]Scholars such as Lin Zhida, Hu Zhengrong, Liu Hailong, Peng Lan, and Kuang Wenbo On different occasions, either in public speeches or in articles, they called on communication scholars to study basic theories, especially in the new media environment. The author has found through his research that studying information communication based on the philosophy of science[7]

---

[6] Sun Xupei, Where to go for communication research in China, Journalism and Communication Research, 2000. 3

[7] See the discussion in Chapters 2 and 3 for more details on how philosophy of science can be an explanatory possibility for social media.

may provide a new research framework and direction in the face of new media events, new communication phenomena, and new communication forms. This research exploration, on the one hand, responds to the call of domestic and foreign scholars, and on the other hand, provides a complement and enrichment to the theory of social media under the leadership of the previous ones.

Under the impact of social media practices, theories of social media communication are also being explored to keep up with the times, especially useful research on theories at the basic and macro levels. There are three reasons for this exploration. First, from the perspective of the discipline of communication, a set of basic theories with more macroscopic explanatory power is needed. Almost every mature discipline, from its emergence to maturity, has undergone one or more "paradigm revolutions", as Kuhn called them, such as the natural sciences, which have gone through the pre-Medieval search for the origin of things, to the post-Medieval search for experimentation and truth, from Newton's classical mechanics to Einstein's theory of relativity, and from classical mechanics to quantum mechanics. It is believed that the natural sciences will continue to undergo paradigm shifts as they continue to explore; philosophy, for example, has been undergoing paradigm shifts from the pre-Socratic period, to modern philosophy of Descartes, Kant, and others, to modern philosophy of science and the structuralist turn. There are many cases in other disciplines, so I will not repeat them. In short, because the world is constantly changing, the study of the world is also constantly changing, and because people[8] are constantly changing, the study of people is also constantly changing. Be practical and keep up with the times. If we look at the paradigm revolution of the discipline from the perspective of development, we will find that the paradigm of journalism and communication also needs to change with the development of society, although it is not so much a paradigm revolution that changes the world, most of the disciplines in journalism and communication do not appear as a discipline revolution, but rather add bricks to the foundation built by the predecessors, but the innovation of theory is very necessary, and is also the development of the

---

[8] The term "person" here refers to a person in society, not specifically to a person with biological characteristics, and will not be explained in this paper unless otherwise mentioned.

discipline However, theoretical innovation is necessary and is the law of the discipline.

Second, the currently introduced sociology has something to add to the explanatory power of information communication. Media practice expects a richer disciplinary explanation, and the development of the discipline needs more and more comprehensive explanatory perspectives. From the perspective of the mainstream paradigm of communication research, there is a functional paradigm that is effect-oriented, a theoretical paradigm of media environment school that is oriented to media technology, a critical paradigm that reflects on the role of media on society from a macro perspective, and a media science that takes the relationship between media and society as the research direction. It can be said that most of the communication research has been based on sociological interpretation, except for Shannon's information theory and Wiener's cybernetics, which are based on computational science. For example, Professor Zhu Jianhua of the City University of Hong Kong has made many contributions to the paradigm shift in communication, proposing the "zero-sum game theory" in media agenda setting, and in researching the audience and effects of communication in the age of Internet proliferation and intelligence. He has also proposed and used concepts such as the "digital divide index" and "trade-off demand theory. Other recent studies on the impact of technology on social media include Jeffrey T. Hancock's "folk theory" [9] and Manuel Castells' "Network Society". Manuel Castells' "Network Society" theory, etc.In the final analysis, however, most of these theories are still based on the sociological paradigm to explain information dissemination. It is obvious in today's era that when information dissemination meets the Internet and the history of human communication develops to a period dominated by Internet-based online media, mobile media, and social media, traditional communication theories still show a lack of explanatory power. On the one hand, it is necessary to explore the explanatory depth of classical communication theories, and on the other hand, it is necessary to add new explanatory perspectives based on the previous ones. Especially today,

---

[9] DeVito, M. A., Birnholtz, J., Hancock, J. T., French, M., & Liu, S. (2018, April). How people form folk theories of social media feeds and what it means for how we study self-presentation. Paper presented at CHI 2018. Montréal.

when media technology has entered 5G, media content has moved towards holography and VR, and media interconnection has moved towards the interconnection of everything, the limitations and shortcomings of the sociological paradigm in explaining new communication phenomena will become more obvious. A viewpoint shared by our scholar Professor Yan Gongjun is that "communication research returns to combining with information theory, system theory and cybernetics, taking the study of information and its quantity as the core, involving the exploration of the connotation and interrelationship of concepts such as information, information quantity, entropy and negentropy."[10] is actually a desire to enrich the interpretation of communication with scientific methods. In fact, it is the hope that the scientific method will be used to enrich the interpretation of communication science. So not only does the discipline of communication science need new explanatory perspectives, but also beyond traditional sociology, enriching explanatory perspectives becomes an inevitable need for media development.

Thirdly, the study of information communication based on quantum philosophy can be integrated into the theoretical torrent of natural philosophy[11] (classical philosophy of mechanics). The study of information communication is part of the theoretical flood and can add new academic energy to the previous research in communication. Through the study of the traditional foundational theories in the field of communication.[12] Basically, all communication theories in the past were based on the philosophy of logic and classical physics, such as the law of cause and effect, which led to a perfectly controlled "academic pursuit" but still showed flaws in their development. In today's communication practice, there are many new characteristics of information dissemination in terms of content, channels, transmission relations and effects, including "uncertainty", "subjective intervention", "emotional interference" and "discontinuity". There are

---

[10] Yan Gongjun, Rethinking Interdisciplinary Research in Chinese Communication, Journalism, 2007, 4

[11] In this context, "natural philosophy" refers to the Western philosophy with the characteristics of continuity, causality, and conservation from the time before the emergence of quantum mechanics, which is the same meaning later.

[12] For a study and analysis of the basic theory of communication, please see Chapter 1 for details.

communication practices and characteristics with quantum characteristics such as "uncertainty," "subjective intervention," "emotional interference," "discontinuity," "quantum connection," and so on. Such communication practices and characteristics abound in social media communication today, so a new study of information communication based on natural philosophy is needed, and a paradigm supplement based on "quantum philosophy" is needed.

DEFINITION AND EXPLANATION OF PHILOSOPHY OF SCIENCE

From the perspective of communication history, the theoretical study of communication is not static or isolated from natural sciences, it is just one of the hundred gardens of human knowledge, and its theories must also conform to the spirit of the times and to the needs of the systematic structure of other knowledge of the times, and evolve. The philosophy of science is a kind of overall value understanding, through the perspective of the philosophy of science to look at information communication, not only from a historical perspective to take care of the various characteristics of information communication, but also to invoke the natural laws of the philosophy of science to observe information communication, so as to give new inspiration to communication science.

Since the basic idea used in this paper is to view communication under the perspective of philosophy of science, especially social media communication under the perspective of non-classical physics theories such as quantum mechanics, a basic brief overview of the history, concepts, and developmental features of philosophy of science is necessary to better account for the research context.

I. The scientific-philosophical concepts used in this paper

The concept of philosophy of science referred to in this paper adopts Professor An Weifu's definition from East China Normal University: "The conceptual community of science-philosophy, that is, the consensus, co-construction and sharing of certain ideas between scientists and philosophers."[13] There are some similar definitions, for example, in the Encyclopedia of China (Philosophy Volume), edited by Hu Qiaomu and others, the philosophy of science has been summarized as "a discipline that examines science from the perspective of philosophy. It takes scientific activities and scientific theories as the object of study, and mainly explores the basic problems concerning the nature of science, the acquisition and testing of scientific knowledge, the logical results of science, and other

---

[13] An Weifu, Philosophy of Science: A Historical Examination of the Basic Categories, Beijing, Beijing Normal University Press, 2015, Preface, pp. 4-5

aspects of scientific epistemology and scientific methodology."[14] According to Professor An Weifu, "Philosophy of science, in the final analysis, is the dialectical unity of knowing the world and knowing oneself, and philosophy of science is to turn knowledge into wisdom. It includes the interrelated ideological composition of scientific view, world view, philosophical view and cultural view."[15] The American scholar Wartowski offers a similar definition when he says that "in the best and deepest sense of philosophy, a humanist understanding of science is a philosophical understanding of science."[16]

Undoubtedly, the continuous development of science has brought about changes in productivity, and changes in productivity, in turn, have brought about changes in the relations of production, and the joint changes in productivity and relations of production have led the advance of society. From a historical point of view, this change has a coherent characteristic, that is, constant acceleration. From the viewpoint of the history of science, the changes in science and technology have been accelerated. The interval between the enlightenment of science and the change that followed the onset of the Industrial Revolution has become shorter and shorter. From 1453, when Copernicus proposed the heliocentric theory, to 1687, when Newton published "Mathematical Principles of Natural Philosophy", the birth of science, to the 19th century, when natural science entered a period of prosperity, the world was even called "the century of science".[17] And scientific inventions are accelerating, "According to statistics, there were 26 major creative inventions of all kinds in the world in the 16th century, 106 in the 17th century, 156 in the 18th century, 546 in the 19th century, and 961 in the first 50 years of the 20th century; 130 more than the total of

[14] Hu Qiaomu et al, Encyclopedia of China (Philosophy Volume I), Beijing, China Encyclopedia Publishing House, 1987, p. 412

[15] An Weifu, Philosophy of Science: A Historical Examination of the Basic Categories, Beijing, Beijing Normal University Press, 2015, p. 353

[16] Wartowski, Fan Dai-nian et al, Conceptual Foundations of Scientific Thought: An Introduction to the Philosophy of Science, 1989, p. 582.

[17] Liu Xiaoying and Fu Wenxiang, The Spinning World, Henan People's Publishing House, August 1990, p. 3

all human history in 3 million years."[18] From the 1960s onwards, scientific inventions developed even faster, growing not in geometric groups but exponentially. Others estimate that it took 50 years for scientific knowledge to double in the 19th century, 10 years in the middle of the 20th century, 5 years in the 1970s and 3 years in the 1980s. ......The number of mature technologies and patents in the world reached 2 million in the 1990s and is still growing at an annual rate of 15%.[19]As Engels said, "Science develops in direct proportion to the amount of knowledge inherited from the previous generation, so that in the most ordinary cases it also grows geometrically."[20]Society tends toward a rapid flow of information, and the accelerated social information in turn is rushing to accelerate exponentially. The materialized individual cannot keep up with this acceleration, but information is booming with unstoppable momentum. before the scientific revolution of the late 19th and 20th centuries, the brilliant scientist Lorentz sighed deeply about wave-particle duality: "There is no longer a standard of truth, nor do I know what science is, and I really regret that I was not able to die five years before these contradictions appeared. " And the scientific revolution brought people the summons: everything is possible, the scientific revolution made the world once so familiar become so strange again, built on the old world view of people's self-confidence again collapsed, the impact on people's mindset is immeasurable.[21]Therefore, the scientific human culture, "turning knowledge into wisdom", is increasingly needed in our time.

II. What is science

Science and philosophy are twins, embodying inseparable characteristics, both in terms of their history and their ideological connotations. According to Professor An WeiFu, "Philosophy and science,

---

[18] Lin Qingshan, The Renewal of Knowledge from the Development of Newtonian Mechanics,Jianghuai Forum, 1985, 1, cited in: Liu Xiaoying and Fu Wenxiang, The Spinning World, Henan People's Publishing House, August 1990, p. 27
[19] Lu Wei Chuan, Who is the Strong Man of the Future World, China Youth Press 1987, p. 179
[20] The Complete Works of Marx and Engels, vol. 1, p. 621
[21] Liu Xiaoying and Fu Wenxiang, The Spinning World, Henan People's Publishing House, August 1990, p. 10

although each has its own history, were not seen as two different things. Until the late Western philosophy. Even when writing their respective histories, it is impossible not to mention each other, except in certain special cases. For the Western intellectual community, philosophy and science were always seen as the same thing, subordinate to the same activity. The description of the relationship between the history of philosophy and the philosophy of science not only constitutes the main reason for philosophy and its history, but also concerns the discussion of the problems of the history of science."[22]

Scientists have defined science in different ways, depending on their point of view and starting point. According to Maurice Cohen, "Simply put, science is a method that identifies and specifies the methods that can be used to find systematic understanding."[23] According to Moore, science is "a systematic spiritual search by man for true knowledge."[24] According to Dampier, "science can be described as structured knowledge of nature, as the rational study of the relations between the various concepts that express natural phenomena."[25] Professor An WeiFu once concluded that "almost every important thinker has formed his or her view of science from his or her own research agenda. For example, Francis Bacon proposed that 'knowledge is power,' Kant proposed that science is 'a priori synthesis of judgment,' Hegel proposed that science is 'rational self-reflection,' Marx proposed that science is 'the forcefulness of human nature,' Wittgenstein proposes that science is 'the synthesis of all true propositions', Heidegger proposes that science is the 'seat of the pants' embedded in a way of life, Kuhn believes that science is the 'beliefs of a professional community', Brewer argues that science is a system of knowledge that follows a 'strong program', Habermas argues that science is 'ideology', Latour argues that science is the accepted 'facts', etc. "[26]

---

[22] Joamme Waigh and Roger Ariew, 2008:15 P49 cited in Philosophy of science: a historical survey of basic categories, An Weifu, Beijing Normal University Press 2015
[23] Rachkov,Han Bingcheng,Science -- Problems - Structure - Fundamental Principles, Beijing Science Press, 1984, p. 3
[24] Li Shengmin,What is science, Hunan Social Science, 2007, No. 1, p. 2
[25] W.C. Dampier,Li Heng, The History of Science and Its Relation to Philosophy and Religion, Guangxi Normal University Press, 2005, p. 8
[26] An Weifu, Philosophy of Science: A Historical Examination of the Basic Categories, Beijing, Beijing Normal University Press, 2015, p. 27

If science is a systematic spiritual inquiry, which after the 17th century became a representation of the natural sciences, then science should be characterized by four norms, as Professor Merton summarizes science as "four institutionally necessary norms --- universality, communalism, disinterestedness, and methodical skepticism，that constitute the spirituality of modern science. "[27]Reflecting on the characteristics of science, Jaspers also proposes three demarcation criteria for science: first, methodological knowledge; second, compelling knowledge; and third, universal validity.[28]

Science represents progress in the cognition of the world, and is then necessarily ephemeral in nature. Science is not static, nor are scientific research and scientific conclusions static, but each relatively static period of science has developed its own unique research paradigm, which continues to revolutionize itself as understanding progresses, eventually resulting in what Kuhn summarizes as the "revolution of science.After examining Kuhn's philosophy, Rong Li gave the conclusion that "the progress of science cannot be understood simply as a process in which imprecise concepts are gradually replaced by more precise ones, driven by experiment."Thus, Kuhn outlines a "very different view of science" that "emerges from the historical record of scientific research activity itself": science is a dynamic, historical process, and the standards of science are also dynamic and historical. Scientific development is neither a mere accumulation process nor a mere revolution, but alternates between conventional scientific progress and scientific revolution, in which conventional scientific development is the most important. Kuhn's model of scientific development can be expressed as follows: pre-science to conventional science (paradigm formation) → crisis → scientific revolution (paradigm shift) → new conventional science (new paradigm formation) → new crisis ...... and even cyclic iterations.[29]This process also echoes Husserl's words, "Science manifests itself as a historical process of constant convergence and infinite progress."[30]

---

[27] R.K. Merton, Lu Xudong and Lin Juren, Sociology of Science,The Commercial Press, 2004, p. 365.
[28] Menghai,The Concept, Scope and Limits of Science -- On Karl Jaspers' View of Science, Natural Dialectics Letters,March 2007, p. 3
[29] Li Rong, A Study of the Sociological Turn in Kuhn's Philosophy of Science, People's Publishing House, 1st edition, March 2018, pp. 46-47
[30] Dai Jianping, A Brief Discussion of Husserl's Ideas on Philosophy of Science, Scientific echnology and Dialectics, Vol. 1, No. 1, 2005, pp. 51-63

DEFINITION AND EXPLANATION OF INFORMATION

I. Scientific-philosophical explanation of information

Information, simply put, is symbolic consciousness.

Information is a fundamental element of human communication activities and one of the basic concepts of this paper, so it is crucial for the understanding of information to define it.The scientific explanation of information began in 1948 with Shannon's famous article "A Mathematical Theory of Communication", in which Shannon viewed information as "bits". Subsequently, James Gleick, in his book "A Brief History of Information", made a clearer arrangement of human society's understanding of information, with the basic point that information is regarded as a basic unit of scientific research alone, so that it is easier to find the rules of information communication.From a social perspective, people are expanding the use of the concept of information, for example, as Toffler profoundly stated in The Third Wave in 1980, "The third wave is the transition from industrialization to informatization";American scholar John Nesbitt also clearly predicted in 1982 in "Megatrends: 10 New Directions That Will Change Our Lives" that changing from an industrial society to an information society is one of the top 10 trends of the future.

As already mentioned, the main hypothetical starting point of this paper is based on the philosophy of science, from which information communication is considered by introducing a scientific epistemology. Therefore, at the level of basic elements, it is necessary to compare the basic unit in communication: information, with the most fundamental unit in physics.

It is currently believed in theoretical physics that the smallest units that make up the world are fermions such as quarks, and a force that connects matter such as quarks, and this force is collectively known as bosons. Theoretical physics has had a long process of understanding the fundamental units that make up the world, a process that began with particles and continued through quantum and string theory, and the understanding of the characteristics of the fundamental units has continued from mass to superstring theory, M-theory, and this process of understanding is continuing.With a little summary, we will find that the understanding of the basic constituent elements in physics has so far been divided into roughly four types: First, according to Newton and his followers, the smallest unit of the world is a solid particle, which means that no matter what kind of knife is used to cut the smallest unit, it must still be a solid, a particle with mass and traits, in the end.Second, according to the early opponents, the mid-17th century view, dominated by Huygens and others, held that, the basic unit that makes up the world is a non-physical fluctuation, which means that whatever knife is used to cut the smallest unit, at the end of the cut, the entity cannot be cut, so the smallest constituent unit is a fluctuation. The third understanding, as the conclusion of Thomas Young's double-slit experiment in 1807 was repeatedly confirmed, the physics community accepted the statement of wave-particle duality, to the effect that the smallest unit that makes up the world is both wave and matter, and is a regular fluctuation before it is observed by humans,and once observed by humans, it immediately collapses into matter. The smallest unit has the dual properties of both wave and particle before being observed, where human consciousness is involved in the objective description of physics for the first time. The fourth understanding is a developmental theory of quantum theory, or string theory.When introducing string theory, Steven S. Gubser, a professor of physics at Princeton University, said, "String theory claims that the fundamental object of all matter is not a particle, but a string.A string is like a small rubber band, but very thin and very strong. An electron is actually conceived as a string, which vibrates and spins on a very small dimension of length ......In some versions of string theory, an electron is a closed loop of a string. In other versions, it is a part of the string with two endpoints".[31]Therefore, the physicists of string theory believe that the smallest unit that makes up the world is a string that can travel freely through 26 or 10 dimension of space-time[32], a string that has the ability to vibrate.The second superstring theory revolution was followed by physicists

---

[31] Steven·Scott·Gubser, String Theory, Chongqing University Press, Introduction, p. 1

[32] Steven·Scott·Gubser, String Theory, Chongqing University Press, Introduction, p. 3

who proposed film theory, M-theory, etc., but they are also developments of string theory.Since these have little relevance to the discussion in this paper, the first string theory and the second superstring theory will be uniformly referred to as string theory.

These are four ways in which physics recognizes the basic units that make up the world, each with specific characteristics.It is important to emphasize here that although the above four understandings are alternative relationships from the perspective of development, in fact this alternative relationship is not a relationship in which the next one annihilates the previous one, but an inclusive relationship in which the new understanding contains the explanation of the previous one, which can be understood as an expansion of the explanatory scope and a narrowing of the limitations of the previous theory.For example, quantum theory is not an annihilating alternative to classical physics (Newtonian mechanics), but a deeper explanation of classical mechanics, while reconciling the parts that Newtonian mechanics cannot explain.

To summarize briefly, the different perceptions of the basic units that make up the world can be simplified into the following four:

First, the particle theory

Secondly, the fluctuation theory

Third, wave-particle duality

Finally, the string theory

Accordingly, by examining the information in comparison with these four types, we are able to formulate the following four hypotheses, and by testing and analyzing the hypotheses, we are able to draw the basic conclusions.

(i) Four assumptions

1. Information is a material entity; 2. Information is a fluctuation; 3. Information is a wave-particle duality; 4. Information is a multidimensional existence string.

It should be noted that the physical characteristics of information referred to here refer to materialization, such as stones, electric waves, words, etc. Anything that can be perceived by the senses of sight, hearing, smell, taste, and touch is materialized.

(ii) Test and analyze the hypothesis (the hypothesis can be confirmed only if both aspects of "existence mode" and "propagation process" are satisfied)

First, the test and analysis of hypothesis 1 "information is a material entity".

Theoretically speaking, information has the possibility of absolute entity existence, but in the process of communication, information is always attached to some kind of manifestation in the process of communication, and this manifestation is symbols, and symbols exist in material entities, non-material entities, linguistic symbols, non-linguistic symbols and other manifestations, such as a book is information, a sentence is information, a gesture is information, so in the process of communication, information does not completely have entity. Therefore assumption 1 is not valid.

Second, the test and analysis of hypothesis 2 "information is a fluctuation" .

Theoretically, the way of existence of information is a fluctuation, which is fully established, and it can be considered that all expressions in the process of communication can be considered as expressions based on this fluctuation. For example, when a person's thoughts are put into words, or when a person sees the sun in the desert, he can conjure up in his mind the image of "Lonely smoke straight in the desert, The long river of the yen down", and then express it through words, paintings or verbal expressions. But in the process of communication to examine, information is a fluctuation will not hold water, or for example, the sun in the desert, which is a kind of objective existence in the broad sense, itself has information, but the way to become information is to be observed or be further interpreted, that is, someone must see, this information has the possibility of being spread. So the information can exist as a solid or as a wave during the propagation process. Therefore assumption 2 is not valid.

Again, making tests and analysis to hypothesis 3"Information is a wave-particle duality".

The possibility of wave-particle duality in the existence of information is certainly valid, because in real life, information can exist as a solid or as a non-physical fluctuating characteristic, and in the process of propagation also exists in both physical and fluctuating forms. And no falsification argument can be found for this hypothesis so far.

At last, making tests and analysis to hypothesis 4" Information is a multidimensional existence string".

According to the string theory, this hypothesis is a description based on the wave-particle duality, that is, it is a more microscopic description based on the recognition of hypothesis 3, which is a deep description of the "wave-particle duality" of the information, mainly the characteristics of the basic unit and the way of movement. Hypothesis 3 and 4 can be combined to argue

(iii) Basic Conclusion.

According to the above argumentation process, we have a clear conclusion about the basic unit of communication, "information" --- its basic appearance is with "wave-particle duality". In other words, information is a wave when it is not observed by human consciousness, and it is a perceptible entity when human consciousness is involved. This conclusion is also consistent with our communication experience. So, if a definition is given to information it would be, "Information: symbolic consciousness".

II. this article's explanation of consciousness - the collection of rational cognition

Returning to the definition of information: "the symbolization of consciousness". The symbol is a clearer concept of a communicable representational element, which will not be discussed since symbols and their representational meanings are not the focus of this article. In this article, consciousness is the focus of the definition of information, so it needs to be explained as necessary.

(i) Examination of the study of consciousness

In the field of consciousness studies, there have been many attempts to define "consciousness", but it is very difficult to really define it.

"Today's neurological view is that consciousness is not a single, monolithic process. It is becoming increasingly clear to us that consciousness is designed with numerous widely distributed specialized systems and split processes."[33]We saw that it is impossible to define consciousness with objective criteria, but it is possible to describe it according to the needs of different interpretations or theories."In the 5th century B.C. Hippocrates wrote the following words as if contemporary neuroscientists were defining consciousness: "Man should know that joy, pleasure, smiles, a strong body, as well as sorrow, grief, disappointment and lamentation, all come from the brain. Through the brain ...... we gain wisdom and knowledge, we can see, we can hear, we know what is beyond the rules, what is fair, what is bad, what is good, what is sweet, what is nasty ...... Through the same organ, we can also become mad and delirious and allow fear and terror to attack us......"[34] In the 1989 International Dictionary of Psychology, psychologist Stuart Sutherland defines consciousness as awareness: having perceptions, thoughts, and feelings: cognition (awareness). ...... cannot determine what it is, what it does, and why it evolved out of it.[35] Descartes also mentions in his Passions of the Soul that "it is the control of animal instincts through thought, reasoning and will that makes man human."[36] Searle defines consciousness as a series of perceptual states that begin at the moment we awaken from a dreamless sleep and continue throughout the day until the moment we fall asleep again, die, fall into a coma, or

[33] Gazzaniga, M. S., & LeDoux, J. E. (1978). The integrated mind. New York: Plenum Press. p224. cited in Who's in Charge? Free will and the science of the brain, [US] Michael Gazzaniga, Zhejiang People's Publishing House, first edition, July 2013.

[34] Hippocrates (400 B.C.). Hippocratic writings (Francis Adams, Trans.) In M.J. Adler (Ed), The great books of the western world (1952 ed., VoL. 10, p. 159) Chicago: Encyclopeedia Britannica, Inc. p211 cited in Who's in Charge? Free will and the science of the brain, [US] Michael Gazzaniga, Zhejiang People's Publishing House, first edition, July 2013.

[35] Sin, W. C., Haas,K, Ruthazer, E. S.,& Cline, H. T (2002). Dendrite growth increased by visual activity requires NMDA receptor and Rho GTPases. Nature, 419(6906), 475-480. p212. cited in Who's in Charge? Free will and the science of the brain, [US] Michael Gazzaniga, Zhejiang People's Publishing House, first edition, July 2013.

[36] R. Descartes (1647). The Passions of the Soul, in J. Cottingham, R. Stoothoff, and D. Murdoch, eds., The Philosophical Writings of Descartes, vol. 1. Cambridge, Eng- land: Cambridge University Press (1985) 32. cited in Descartes' Errors, [US] Antonio Damasio, Beijing Union Publishing Company, 1st edition, February 2018

are in some other "unconscious state" .The series of perceptual states in between can be collectively referred to as "states of consciousness"(Searle, 1998, p. 1936).[37] Therefore, he considered consciousness as a higher-level special property expressed by the process of specific neural activity. After the natural philosophical turn in the understanding of consciousness, the view, represented by Crick and Qiu Qimei, is that "consciousness is a product of particular neural activity".Psychology considers consciousness as a sum of feelings; philosophy of mind considers consciousness as an innate rationality related to the mind; philosophy of science considers consciousness as an organismic response, In short, although the definition of consciousness varies widely from discipline to discipline and from research path to research path, one thing is clear: consciousness is a collection of perceptions. It can be described according to different explanatory needs.

(ii) Can only describe, not define

Many scholars have taken a dim view of the ability to define the concept of consciousness accurately. For example, C. McGinn argues that human scientific inquiry may never be able to deal with the hard problem of consciousness because it is beyond our understanding; D. Papineau even argues that the whole scheme of finding neural correlates of conscious activity (NCC) by scientific means is wrong; F. Crick and C. Koch) argue that in today's arena of consciousness research, a wise philosopher should step aside.[38]In fact, the core of the problem of consciousness is to solve the problem of "body-mind" relationship.

There are currently two more popular approaches in the field of consciousness studies. One is the research path based on the philosophy of mind, which is the understanding of consciousness based on Descartes' mind-body dualism. "In traditional philosophy, free will is the belief that human behavior is an expression of personal choice and is not

---

[37] Wang Xiaoyang, Studies in Consciousness, Shanghai People's Publishing House, April 2019, p. 4
[38] Wang Xiaoyang, Studies in Consciousness, Shanghai People's Publishing House, April 2019, pp. 1-2

determined by physical factors, fate, or the godhead."[39]The main thrust of his philosophy is the idea that there is an independent conscious existence, and that although it is related to the body and the environment in one way or another, consciousness is relatively independent of the body and consciousness is free. Descartes once said, "I first tried to discover in general the origin or cause of everything that exists or could exist in the world, without considering anything else that could serve this purpose except God Himself who has created this world, or without deducing these origins or causes from any other source than some germ of truth that naturally exists in our souls. "[40]However, the rebuttal to this claim is also sharper, as John Locke says: "The will really signifies nothing more than a power or ability to like or choose. If one thinks of the will in terms of faculty, rather than in terms of the ability to do something, it would be absurd to say that it is free or not."[41]The second is a research path based on brain neuroscience (cognitive neuroscience), to the effect that consciousness is not recognized as existing independently of the body, and that the body is standardized as a research domain of brain neuroscience. Expressing consciousness through descriptions of brain structures, brain nerves and information or energy interactions in the brain, this progression has gained a slight upper hand in the field of consciousness research in recent years for reasons of scientific validity[42], repeatable tests, and so on. The study is also divided into two research approaches, one is the constructive block

[39] Michael Gazzaniga, Who's in Charge? Free will and the science of the brain, Zhejiang People's Publishing House, July 2013, p. 102

[40] René Descartes L, Meditations on the Supreme Philosophy, Collected Philosophical Works of Descartes, compiled, E. S. Holden and G. R. T. Ross (New York: Dover Publications, 1955 English edition), vol. 1, p. 154

[41] Locke, J. (1689). An essay concerning human understanding (1849 ed., p. 155). Philadelphia : Kay&Troutman.P227P227 Cited in Who's in Charge? Free will and the science of the brain, Michael Gazzaniga, Zhejiang People's Publishing House, July 2013, 1st edition.

[42] The term "scientific" here refers to the scientific nature of the research method, and is neutral in nature.

approach and the other is the unified field approach,[43]The work that has dominated the field is the famous book Descartes' Error, written by the famous American brain neuroscientist Antonioni Damasio.Of course, strictly speaking, there is also a third research path, because this path advocates not to study what consciousness is, but to use consciousness as a universally agreed concept, such as Zhao Tingyang's saying that "the world is what consciousness is", and generally does not pursue conceptual accuracy, but only uses universal consciousness perception as the discourse element of his research. However, since we are going to do a conceptual investigation in this paper, we will leave the third way out for now.

However, there is a certain consensus in both philosophy of mind and neuroscience: there is definitely a connection between "neurological activity" and "human consciousness". If it is difficult to distinguish between physical dynamics and independent consciousness, we can start with the study of the relationship between consciousness and neurological activity by seeking common ground while preserving differences.Therefore, most of the current research in the field of consciousness studies has chosen the research path of "setting aside the controversy and developing together", which tends to "describe but not define" consciousness.On the road of describing consciousness, from the dualism of mind and body to the research of "conscious experience" represented by Negel and Jackson, to the research of easy and difficult problems by Chalmers,turn from the "naturalistic" proposed by Searle to the stimulus response theory insisted by

---

[43] Note: "Unified field" is originally a physical concept, in scientific research, whether in natural science or social science, there are different people in different periods of time to pursue a "unified field", and very often, the pursuit of a unified field has become the belief of a certain generation or a certain scientist.Some hope to unify multiple theories into a single theory, such as Einstein's pursuit of a unified field theory of physics in his later years, while others are able to reconcile incompatible theories in the same field as soon as they appear, such as Riemannian geometry (non-Euclidean geometry) in geometry, which can be understood as the ascension of the spatio-temporal dimension if considered from the dimensional point of view of physics (mentioned later), or the re-recognition after dialectic if considered from the philosophical point of view.

Damasio and others, and now to the direction of quantum consciousness[44] represented by Penrose and Hameroff, as well as the more cutting-edge "supercomputer" explanation based on artificial intelligence and so on.

(iii) Consciousness and its characteristics in the perspective of philosophy of science

The concept of consciousness used in this paper is a philosophical definition under the field of brain neuroscience, consciousness: a collection of rational cognition. This cognition includes emotional, affective, rational and other mental activities, which are subject to the external environment to construct a field. Since the concept of "consciousness" in this paper is a basic component of information (symbolic consciousness), which is a very important force in the process of information dissemination, and information is the basic concept of this paper, it is necessary to explain and clarify the concept of "consciousness" chosen for this paper.

The view of this paper is, first, that the choice of the definition of consciousness by brain neuroscience is consistent with the basic observation perspective of the philosophy of science in this paper. Second, the brain neuroscience explanation of consciousness is scientifically valid and convincing.

Early on, a group of scientists argued that The purely independent existence of such mental concepts as "consciousness," "mind," "heart," and "creativity" by Plato and Descartes was not possible. In "Civilization and [ts Discontens]", Freud introduced the concept of the "superego", arguing that It is the "superego" that subordinates instincts to social norms. This view is a leap forward from Descartes' dualism, but it lacks a clear neural mechanism.[45] Damasio goes further, saying, "Our growing understanding of the external world can be seen as an adjustment that occurs in the

---

[44] The starting point of "quantum consciousness" is that they believe that traditional neuroscience cannot finally explain the properties of consciousness, and that quantum mechanics, which describes the basic behavior of matter and energy, must be introduced. Quoted in Wang Xiaoyang, "Consciousness Research", Shanghai People's Publishing House.

[45] S. Freud (1930). Civilization and Its Discontents. Chicago: University of Chicago Press. cited in Descartes' Errors, [US]Antonio Damasio, Beijing Union Publishing Company, 1st edition, February 2018

neural space in which the body and brain interact. Not only is the idea that mind and brain are separate a conjecture, but the idea that body and mind are separate from each other may also be a pipe dream. In the full sense of mind, the mind is embedded not only in the brain but also in the soma."[46]Leo Szilad, a physicist and biologist, has the opinion that creative scientists, artists and poets have something in common. Logical thinking and analytical skills are necessary abilities for scientists, but only these two are not enough to do creative work. Scientific inspiration does not come from logical deduction of existing knowledge; creative work of scientific significance relies on activity at the subconscious level.Jonas Salk shares hold the same view and believes that creativity is based on "the fusion of intuition and reasoning".[47]The brain neuroscientist Gazzaniga further argues that "we now envision that there are multiple systems in the human brain, some distributed in the left half of the brain and some in the right half. We no longer think that the brain is entirely divided into two consciousness systems; instead, we think it consists of multiple dynamic mental systems. …....The general view is as follows:We have multiple layers of emergent systems, from the particle-physical layer to the atomic-physical layer, to the chemical layer, to the biochemical layer, to the cellular-biological layer, to the physiological layer, and finally to the mental processing."[48]

In brain neuroscience, consciousness is often segmented into aspects such as emotions and behavior, and the overall way of movement within the brain can again be unified into the interaction of electrical currents. Scientists in the field have demonstrated experimentally that intracerebral activity precedes consciousness. They generally believe that the brain is composed of numerous modules that form a complete unity, bringing about a clear, natural flow of consciousness, and that the brain completes the construction between sensation, emotion, memory, and action through the interaction of electrical currents."The brain activity involved

---

[46] Antonio Damasio, Descartes' Error, Beijing Union Publishing Company, 1st edition, February 2018, p. 116

[47] Antonio Damasio, Descartes' Error, Beijing Union Publishing Company, 1st edition, February 2018, p. 181

[48] Michael Gazzaniga, Who's in Charge? Free will and the science of the brain, Zhejiang People's Publishing House, July 2013, p. 55

in initiating an action (such as pressing a button) occurs 500 milliseconds before that action. This certainly makes sense. But surprisingly, subjects reported action-related brain activity 300 milliseconds before there was conscious awareness of the action. The accumulation of charge within the brain precedes the conscious decision, which is called the 'pre-motion preparation potential', or simply 'preparation potential'"[49]In 2008, John-Dylan Haynes and colleagues extended Libet's experiments to reveal that brain activity can encode the outcome of a behavioral tendency for up to 10 minutes before allowing it to enter consciousness! The brain is active first, and the person becomes conscious afterwards.[50]Harvard researchers Alfonso Caramazza and Jennifer Shelton have shown through their research that the brain has specific knowledge systems for animate and inanimate objects, which have different neural mechanisms. These domain-specific knowledge systems are not knowledge per se; their purpose is to allow you to notice specific aspects of your environment, thereby increasing the probability of human survival.[51]It is clear that the intracerebral system is a "behavioral shortcut" based on the premise of survival to judge the environment and learn to cope with it. If the previous study only proved that behavior precedes consciousness, but not the relationship between behavior and mind, Damasio proved conclusively through experiments that behavior is a determinant of consciousness. He himself raised the above question, "There is behavior not necessarily mind ...... Many simple organisms, even with only one cell and no brain, can produce spontaneous behavior or respond to environmental stimuli, that is, these organisms produce behavior. "[52]The following are some excerpts from the book Descartes' Errors to demonstrate the logic of his research.

[49] Libet, B., Gleason, C. A. Wright, E. W.,& Pearl, D.K.(1983). Time of conscious intention to act in relation to onset of cerebral activity (readinesspotential): The unconscious initiation of a freely voluntary act. Brain. 106(3), 623-642.P226 cited in Who's in Charge? Free will and the science of the brainl, [US] Michael Gazzaniga, Zhejiang People's Publishing House, first edition, July 2013
[50] Michael Gazzaniga, Who's in Charge? Free will and the science of the brain, Zhejiang People's Publishing House, July 2013, p. 120
[51] Michael Gazzaniga,Who's in Charge? Free will and the science of the brain, Zhejiang People's Publishing House, July 2013, p. 45
[52] Antonio Damasio, Descartes' Error, Beijing United Publishing Company, 1st edition, February 2018

"I believe that emotions and feelings are at the heart of rationality, and that both are important manifestations of drives and instincts and are a major part of how drives and instincts operate."

"Having a mind means that the organism has generated neural representations that can form representations, which are processed through thought processes and ultimately influence behavior by helping the organism predict the future, make plans, and choose next actions."

"The strong sense that we always think the mind is one stems from the cooperation of a large range of neural systems, and synchronized neural activity in different brain regions at the anatomical level contributes to this illusion."

"The factual knowledge required for reasoning and decision making originates in the mind and exists in the form of representations."[53]

According to Damasio, behavior is a survival choice, a collection of behaviors is a rational behavior, a collection of multiple rational behaviors forms rapid response patterns, a collection of these response patterns becomes emotions, emotions, and other mind, and mind forms consciousness. Paul Weiss, one of the first developmental neurobiologists, provided more evidence for the concept of equipotentiality. He also believes that "function comes before form."[54]Gazzaniga shares this view "This is because there is overwhelming evidence that brain function is automated and that our experience of consciousness is an afterthought."[55]So we all tend to generate or learn survival behaviors first, then form what is called perceptual awareness such as emotions, and eventually consciousness.

According to brain neuroscience scientists, consciousness is a collection of "shortcuts" after the game of survival, seemingly emotional emotions, but actually rational "shortcuts".

[53] Antonio Damasio, Descartes' errors,Beijing Union Publishing Company, 1st edition, February 2018, pp. 90, 91, 96, 97, 114

[54] Weiss, P. A. (1934).In vitro experiments on the factors determining the course of the outgrowing nerve fiber. Journal Experimental Zoology, 68(3), 393-448 P211 cited in Who's in Charge? Free will and the science of the brain, [US] Michael Gazzaniga, Zhejiang People's Publishing House, July 2013, first edition

[55] Michael Gazzaniga, Who's in Charge? Free will and the science of the brain, Zhejiang People's Publishing House,July 2013, p. 119

(iv) Definition and characteristics of the consciousness used in this paper

It is clear from the above that the two dominant progressions of consciousness boil down to the question of whether matter determines consciousness or consciousness determines matter. The question of matter and consciousness has not been able to be convincingly stated, or unified. Research in theoretical physics has led to the recognition of the wave-particle duality of the smallest unit of the world from double-slit interference experiments, and the first evidence of the involvement of consciousness in the conversion of waves to particles, with consciousness clearly characterized as a force.The study of consciousness also provides experimental proof that consciousness determines the form of matter. By examining the smallest particles in physics, we will find an interesting phenomenon that there is enough evidence in our world that the smallest matter is of particles, and there is also enough advanced evidence that the tiniest unit that makes up the world is the wave, and it is human consciousness that makes the wave into a particle, and wave-particle duality, a very strange contradiction, also gives sufficient arguments for consciousness to determine matter.But with the development of physics, the research of quantum mechanics has carried out the revolution of string theory and superstring theory, which can be understood to the effect that the tiniest unit that makes up our world is a string, or a string that exists in higher dimensions and unfolds in lower dimensions, and even time is only the unfolding of higher dimensions in four-dimensional space-time, giving us a philosophical summary that in fact, if we encounter a pair of conclusions that are each justified, and still contradictory, we can look at the problem in a higher dimension. The philosophical summary for us is that if we are confronted with a pair of conclusions that are both valid and contradictory, we can take a higher dimensional view of the problem, and string theory takes this higher dimension from a physical point of view.

So when we look at consciousness, we see that the relationship between consciousness and matter is a typical contradiction, and quantum mechanics has proven that consciousness has the characteristics of "force", so we can make the following assumption: the consciousness we know is a four-dimensional space-time unfolding of a force in a higher dimensional space. It is determined by matter in higher dimensions, but it cannot be fully described in the four-dimensional space-time in which we live.

Relying on the above assumptions, since information is a symbolization of consciousness, it has the following characteristics:

1. Information can be transmitted over distance because consciousness exists in higher dimensions, so the information attached to the symbols has high-dimensional characteristics in itself when it is not transmitted.

2. Information is presented in four-dimensional spacetime with uncertainty. According to quantum mechanics and string theory, all observed fundamental units of matter are probability sets, so information can also be assumed as the presentation of higher dimensional spacetime in four-dimensional spacetime, except that this weekly presentation itself is probabilistic, that is, uncertainty is the basic characteristic of information.

3. The composition of information can be assumed to be the compositional structure of the smallest atom. There are two kinds of smallest units that make up the atom, one is the fermion with solid characteristics, and the other is the boson without solid but with force characteristics, both of them together make up the atom, if the hypothesis about information in this paper is valid, then the symbol can be understood as the "fermion" that makes up the information, and the consciousness can be understood as the "boson" that plays the role of connection. "In physics, bosons also have the property that they can overlap in a space, which is very similar to the role of consciousness in information.

So we can simply conclude that information is highly dimensional and uncertain, and that awareness as a force runs through the entire process of information composition and information communication. This definition of information proposed in this paper will be further discussed and validated in the full-text social media study.

METHODOLOGY, STRUCTURE
AND INNOVATION USED
IN THIS STUDY

I. The Methods Used in This Study

This paper focuses on literature research methods, classification and exclusion methods, empirical and case study methods, comparative methods, interview methods, and crawler-based computer-aided analysis.

Literature Research is a method of collecting, organizing, studying, and analyzing literature to develop a scientific understanding of the facts under discussion. The advantages of literature research are low cost, large coverage, focus on the topic, and suitability for macro and longitudinal analysis. Classification is a scientific method of grouping things together (with similar characteristics). By comparing the similarities between things and grouping things with certain common points or similar characteristics into an indefinite set, a large amount of complicated materials can be organized and systematized, so as to discover the laws of things and provide guidance for understanding specific things.The so-called exclusion method, also called elimination method, is a way to provide indirect proof, which is a way to exclude the existence of false propositions based on analogical comparison and feasibility, and can be used in combination with the classification method. The so-called empirical research is a method of research that is carried out through data collection in order to formulate and test theoretical hypotheses. The most important empirical research is Case Study, which is a research method that starts from a typical case in a certain aspect to examine, describe and explain the general characteristics and rules of things in a thorough and comprehensive way. The comparative method is to understand things by observing, analyzing, and finding out the similarities and differences of the object of study. Interview is a basic research method to understand the psychology and behavior of the interviewees through face-to-face conversation. Computer-assisted content analysis based on crawlers, on the other hand, is a content analysis technique based on the application of computer technology, which helps qualitative and quantitative research under big data.

This paper adopts a combination of the above methods, such as using more literature, classification and exclusion methods in the theoretical part, and more case studies and computer-aided analysis in the empirical research part, so that the purpose of the study can be better achieved.

II. Structure of this paper

The macro structure of this paper consists of an introductory section and six chapters in the main part. In the introductory part, which mainly raises questions and clarifies concepts, this paper argues that social media has become the main mode of communication in today's society, and the existence of information and communication has changed dramatically, while the traditional theoretical explanatory power is insufficient for social media, and the explanation of philosophy of science should be introduced. The introductory part defines and discusses the two basic concepts of philosophy of science and information, especially Consciousness in the concept of information is discussed and studied. In the six chapters of the main text, the first chapter of this paper, firstly, starts from the development of social media and the dilemma of theoretical explanation, and further raises questions in a macro perspective; the second chapter of this paper presents the new characteristics of social media in communication from the perspective of the development of media technology, the changes of traditional communication elements and the creation of new communication elements; the third chapter is an attempt to explain with the basic concepts and methods of philosophy of science These new communication elements and characteristics; Chapter 4 is an attempt to establish a new scientific-philosophical explanation system about social media; Chapter 5 is an attempt to explain the status, role, and new characteristics embodied by social media in communication through some latest specific cases, including the public opinion storm caused by the 2019 British death van, the French yellow vest movement, and the incident of the NBA president's inappropriate remarks involving China in the United States, thus to verify our above theoretical explanation of the philosophy of science. The last chapter is a conclusion, which summarizes the findings while pointing out the shortcomings in the study and the directions for further research.

III. The innovation point and difficulty in this paper

(i) Perspective innovation

We will break the linear communication perspective proposed by Lasswell since 1948 and build a spatio-temporal communication perspective based on the philosophy of science; we will break the conservative research of point-by-point transformation of communication studies and build a systematic explanation system; we will break the sociological perspective of global social media communication and build a new scientific research framework.

(ii) Theoretical innovation

There are three main levels.At the macro level, the main purpose is to establish a new interpretation system of communication under the concept of philosophy of science; at the meso level, it is to establish six scientific interpretation units corresponding to the six elements of new communication in social media under the introduction of the research results of quantum mechanics;at the micro level, it is to establish a more reasonable and explanatory operation method through the explanatory system and explanatory units corresponding to specific communication practices in a specific case study, so as to establish an explanatory framework in the case study.

(iii) The theoretical difficulty lies in the establishment of the explanatory system

The main difficulty of this paper does not lie in the explanation, but in the establishment of the explanation system, that is, how to use the understanding system of the philosophy of science to connect science and sociology and establish many explanation units, and at the same time to sort out the explanation units into an explanation system that can have the up and down relationship.

(iv) Reconciliation difficulty

The problem of reconciling symbolic formulas with social disciplines is a natural obstacle that cannot be calculated with complete precision. That is, how to organically combine the abstraction of theory with the richness of reality. In this paper, some abstract offices are proposed, but both "E=MhV2", which expresses the effect of propagation, and the integral derivative formula, the final result is symbolic and cannot enter into mathematical and theoretical calculations accurately. It can be argued that the formulas studied in conjunction with social sciences are difficult to express mathematically, and cannot be verified precisely in the laboratory like the natural sciences, but can only express traits, logic and trends. This is also determined by the characteristics of social sciences, and what we can do in this paper is to try to make it seem reasonable, self-consistent and logical.

CHAPTER 1

RETHINKING COMMUNICATION PRACTICES AND THEORETICAL EXPLANATIONS OF GLOBAL SOCIAL MEDIA

In the introduction of this paper, it has been suggested that traditional communication theory faces challenges in the new communication practice. The question to be addressed in this chapter is why traditional communication theory is said to face new challenges? What are the changes that have taken place in the development of communication practice, especially the latest iterations of media, and what do they bring to the table? It also addresses the question of why this paper proposes a philosophy of science approach to thinking about communication, and what new directions this can take us?

RETHINKING TRADITIONAL COMMUNICATION RESEARCH

In recent years, society has rapidly entered a new information age, from the initial informationization in the second half of the last century to a high degree of informationization after the 1990s, and some believe that a fourth industry has even been formed in addition to the traditional primary, secondary and tertiary industries. The highly informatized society has made the concepts of "social media," "5G," "smart media," "Internet of Everything," "virtual reality", and so on have gradually turned from jargon and prospect into reality and entered human society. The development of communication practice provides a bigger stage for communication research on the one hand, and presents a more serious challenge on the other.

Communication science emerged at the dawn of the information society in the 1940s and 1950s, and formed its own independent disciplinary discourse much earlier, nearly a century ago now.In the process, the positivist school, the critical school, and the technical school (media environment school) have become the three schools of thought. However, in terms of the basic theory of communication, there seems to be a lack of philosophical answers to the questions of "who am I", "where do I come from" and "where do I go".

The lack of basic theory in China has been explored by many scholars. In 1994, Mr. Lin Zhida pointed out in his book "Research on the Basic Theory of Communication" that the confusion of communication disciplines and the blind crossover of research were due to the lack of a solid basic theory in communication. 2010, Professor Yuan Jinghua summarized this sense of responsibility and mission of the discipline's development that could not keep up with the changes of the times as: the anxiety of self-perception of the discipline's identity and the crisis of autonomy.In 2011, Professor Hu Zhengrong also expressed his concerns and expectations in his article "Reflection and Transcendence: A Ten-Year Review of Chinese Communication Research", and in 2016, Professor Shao Peiren of Zhejiang University published "From Ideas to Theories: On the Possible Paths for the Construction of Local Communication Theories", in which he categorized China's "self-developed" and "self-defined" communication theories into"two schools and three sects" in an attempt to summarize, while emphasizing the continuous appeal of communication scholars, including Professor Hu Zhengrong, for "independent research and development" of communication theory.

In the face of the call for theoretical innovation in communication, and since the source of communication is interdisciplinarity, this paper tries to find some answers from the philosophy of science, especially from the philosophical thinking of quantum mechanics. Although in 2007, Professor Yan Gongjun proposed his thoughts on interdisciplinary research in his article "Rethinking Interdisciplinary Research in Chinese Communication", he also proposed valuable ideas on the combination of natural sciences such as "entropy" and information theory with communication.In recent years, among the studies on new communication interpretation, there are Professor Yu Guoming's exploration of high-dimensional media, scholars such as Bian Donglei of Nanjing University and Shao Peiren of Zhejiang University who have worked on the issue of media time. It can be said that the cutting-edge thinking of many researchers is the basis and motivation for the author to write this thesis. For communication science, understanding and explaining through the philosophy of science, especially quantum mechanics, may sound like an "academic game", but in the Internet era, it may be an "academic fate" that has to be thought and explained. Let's take this kind of argument or explanation as a new attempt, and I think that this kind of effort is necessary and possible, even as a kind of "trial and error", it is also meaningful.

I. The development of communication theory is trapped in the research ideas, framework and methods laid down in the early days

The important ground for the formation of the discipline of communication was the formation of mass communication in the late 19th and early 20th centuries, the rapid development of the media in the first half of the 20th century and the widespread recognition of the influence of communication, especially stimulated by the "propaganda war" of World War I and the "general war" of World War II.The theoretical study of communication was formerly inherited from the intersection of sociology, journalism, psychology and other disciplines, and was organized and independent by scholars such as Lasswell and Schramm, and finally became a lineage.

From the starting point of research, communication science has an innate gene that is fully compatible with media practice. It can be said that in the vast majority of cases, the study of communication and media practice are in a parasitic relationship, with media practice giving important nutrients and materials to communication research and maintaining a research sequence in which practice leads theory. Since the founding father, Schramm, wanted to demonstrate the continuity and scientific nature of the discipline at its inception, he cited four sociologists as pioneers of communication and integrated all their experiments and studies involving the concept of communication into the initial communication theory, placing the practicality and functionality of communication at the forefront of research from the very beginning of the discipline.Under this premise, communication science has laid down the traditional gene of research effects and practical methodology over basic theory induction. Especially after the establishment of communication science, the period of rapid media development and the entry of human beings into the information age, no one was overly concerned about the fundamental integrity and scientific nature of the discipline due to its high degree of fit with practice, and even though some scholars questioned whether it was a discipline, they were all lost in history by the public's expectations for communication research. Therefore, the basic starting point of the discipline's early practice led research has become a reasonable logic recognized by communication scholars, and this is the basic path that communication research has not bypassed to this day.

The theoretical foundation of communication studies is the linear 5W model guiding categorical research, which, although very useful in practice, has become a cage of thinking that shackles communication studies to break through. Lasswell proposed the 5W theory, which very cleverly framed the study of communication into the framework of cybernetics, audience research, content research, media research, and effect research, and even though the 5W theory has been revised in later generations, it has not been separated from the cage of these five research directions. In fact, this theory is actually a methodology rather than

4

a basic theory.This theory has both advantages and disadvantages. On the plus side, the five research directions seem to make communication research more structured, with clear research subdivision perspectives, and satisfy society's desire for a systematic study of communication.In terms of disadvantages, the 5W communication model has laid down a way of thinking, and classification studies are popular to this day, knowing only the division but not the combination, knowing only the part regardless of the whole, narrowing the communication in the scope of the plane division,so that there is even a blind crossover of disciplines in later studies, such as health communication, computer communication, and other fancy things, without debating connotations and extensions.However, there is nothing wrong with crossover, but the crossover must be supported by the solid basic theory of the discipline, otherwise it will appear that the more crossover, the more unclear the situation.This explains why the vitality of most cross-sectional research in communication is quite similar to that of seafood --- fresh, but cannot keep fresh easily.Now revisit McGuire and Wendell co-authored the book "Mass Communication Model Theory" listed in more than 40 major communication models, also all reveal the word "split". Therefore, the result of the splitting of the communication plane is that the horizontal expansion, attacking the city, killing the four sides, while the vertical depth, the roots are not deep, difficult to resist the wind and waves.

The over-reliance on pragmatism has led to a tendency toward a somewhat quick-impact effectivism, and an over-reliance on quantitative research, even based solely on data, has led communication research to become segmented and data-dependent over time. For example, one of the guiding studies of the positivist school is the Erie County survey led by Lazarsfeld, whose "two-level theory of communication" and "limited effects" theory, although highly questionable, is still the It is still an introductory theory to communication studies today.There are many untenable points in the theory. For example, the two-level communication theory, for one thing, this conclusion is intended to explore the inevitability of cascading influence, which at first glance makes sense, influencing influential people and then influencing others, but take a closer look at the conclusion, that reached has gone beyond the answer that its experimental data can give, and it is difficult to conclude whether communication has a cascade. Second, the choice of the object of study is too isolated, and the conclusion that the impact of communication on the audience is limited in a specific time, scope, and scope of a specific event has itself been qualified out of the practical test of communication. Third, from the perspective of the larger communication environment, the media has been influencing all aspects of society for a long time since the 1930s, such as the Erie County survey, which is regarded as a classic study of communication, Erie County has long been influenced in the larger media environment, so the Lazarsfeld team subjectively ignored the long-term social images of regional audiences, there is some suspicion of generalization. However, the quantitative argument is so strong that it is difficult to argue with the data, which has shaped the research path of most communication scholars who rely on data to argue for effects in later years.

Communication research methods are overly influenced by quantitative research methods in sociology. The idea that "if you take on its mantle, you must believe in its method" is deeply implanted. Quantitative research in sociology is a complementary approach with corroborative function, and its rigor is not proven to be self-refuting, only because there is no better alternative method, it is cited as the basis. Moreover, a mature discipline should have not only a basic disciplinary level and professional level in its methodology, but also a philosophical level. However, this method has been used to date because of its extensive use by leading communication scholars and because most of the results of this method can be optimized at will according to the research objectives. This method and the data it produces can only be used as supporting evidence, and it is very difficult to draw accurate conclusions or even to summarize solid theories based on this research method alone.

II. Applied communication cannot be supported by the basic theory of communication

Every time a new form of media emerges, it is a challenge to communication theory, which is both embarrassing and exciting. The embarrassment lies in the fact that one or several previous media theories have to be used to explain the new media practices, while the excitement lies in the fact that one can build or improve one's own theoretical system according to the new object of study. Because there is no unified theoretical foundation for communication, and because it is more or less dependent on certain established disciplines for cross-studies or under emerging industries, communication has always shown that it cannot survive on its own. Because of the lack of a unique basic theory, it also seems to follow the same trend and lacks independent spirit in its relationship with applied practice . The most representative one is the naming of emerging media. The variety and confusion of nomenclature not only reveals the weakness of the foundation of communication research, but also reveals the problem of not being able to accurately describe the operation of emerging media.

From a theoretical point of view, communication research is mostly partial and unable to form a systematic logic, mostly extended by the 5W classification logic, and interspersed with a variety of subdivisions combined with the phenomenon, and its research results mostly show a "partially reasonable" characteristic. When it comes to application, it is not working well, especially in today's highly developed information society. For example, the problem of gatekeeper theory failure in the new media era, the emergence of dynamic gatekeeper and other revisionist theories, is still mostly conceptual, and does not see the fixed attribute of gatekeeper as the representative of information interests.In the period of point-to-point media such as TV and newspapers, the concept of "gatekeeper" emerged because of the monopoly of the information communication system and the fact that information must be processed and handled by people in the process of communication, but in the era of relatively free communition of network media, information receivers and communicater are free to switch, the frequency of information interaction is intensified, and the channels of news production are diversified., and the issue of information control, media organizations and information interaction platforms are gradually changing, and the hotness of the two microblogs is gradually proving that the identity and role of traditional gatekeepers are changing, and the concept of gatekeeper is stretched in guiding practice.For example, in the news at the end of the popular network in today's society, there is a situation that social opinion is generated based on emotions but not on facts, and the phenomenon that truth is hard to find, reversal of public opinion is common, and social consensus disappears.For example, "Brexit", "Trump's election", "French yellow vest" movement, etc.In 2016, Oxford

Dictionaries summarized these phenomena of swaying public opinion based on emotions, feelings, and beliefs into a new word: "post-truth (post-truth)"Contemporary communication practice has broken the bottom line of fact-based journalism theory and challenged the theory of communication. The original theory of audience analysis is not sufficient to solve the emerging problems, and the theory describing audience emotions is not sufficient to explain the role played by the media, and there is no clear prediction on what theory this phenomenon is based on and where the future direction will be.Therefore, in the face of new media practices, communication theory will certainly face not the continued outward expansion of multiple theories to bring new interpretations, but the integration and systematization of multiple theories, which is the only way to better respond to the test brought by the development of media practices.

The rapid development of media and the insufficient follow-up of theoretical studies have led to the blindness of society in naming media. In a mature discipline system, the period of practice and its naming should conform to its regularity of the categorical standard. Because communication science started late and the laws of communication are still being explored, the naming of media in different periods is mostly based on the common usage of the public or simple summary of phenomena. This is very common in communication practice, for example, naming media by the name of the carrier, such as newspaper media, radio media, TV media, etc.; or naming them by their physical representation, such as print media, electronic media, etc.; or naming them by the space they are in, such as outdoor media, building media, in-vehicle media; or naming them by the functions they perform in society, such as social media, interactive media, etc.; or simply naming media that cannot be categorized in a uniform way at all as all-media, convergent media, multi-media, etc. At the research level, what is most unacceptable is the provisionality and inaccurate. Nature of the media phenomenon and research in the past 30 years, a characteristic has emerged, that is, the media that cannot be named are all prefixed with the name of new media.It is subsequently prefixed by the name of the carrier or emergent space, and later by the social function it embodies.Such as new media to network media to social media, the lamentable thing is that, due to the rapid change of carriers in the past two decades, many people are confused about what exactly is the new media. This phenomenon reflects the inaccuracy of communication studies and the fact that the development of media vehicles is completely outside the scope of existing communication laws.

In 1994, the Internet became commercially available, and in 1998, the Internet was recognized as the "fourth media" by the United Nations, and at the same time the Internet was introduced into China. The accelerated integration of media and society has led to a new wave of theoretical exploration, as well as the exploration of tinkering with mass communication theory. With the rapid iteration of carriers, it is one patch after another, and the rapidity of change is overwhelming. Especially in today's society, social media has become the most important media channel for information dissemination. In global communication activities, social media can be seen in almost all influential communication practices, and even assume the role of the most important communication leader. However, most of the academic explanations for these new communication phenomena are still based on the tinkering with the theoretical framework of communication in the past. Although some concepts are beginning to be borrowed from sociology, psychology, political science and even natural science, and some concepts have been innovated, such as "empowerment theory," "scenario theory," "self-organization theory ","High-dimensional media",etc.Although these explanations have, to a certain extent, alleviated the embarrassing situation that theory cannot keep up with practice, there is still room for further research and exploration, especially in forming a basic theory and a complete explanation system.These theories do not fundamentally address the fundamental theoretical issues in the new communication environment, and it is difficult to fundamentally solve the problems. The current deep integration of media and society urgently signals the need for fundamental changes in media theory to adapt to social development. The study of social media communication theory may need to be approached from a new perspective to establish a system with scientific and complete the system of explanatory and predictive capabilities. This is the reason why this dissertation attempts to draw on the philosophy of science and the latest results of the fusion of natural science and sociology to sort out a perspective and method that has universal explanatory power for global social media communication.

DEVELOPMENT OF COMMUNICATION PRACTICES:INSIGHTS FROM THE EIGHT COMMUNICATION REVOLUTIONS

Communication is a human instinct, a basic human need, and a need for human production, life and their own reproduction and development. The content of communication is information, "man himself is an information processor", [56]with the continuous updating of communication tools, human communication methods, content and the impact of communication on society is also changing.

I. The history of information communication: eight information revolutions

The communication of information in human society has been around for a long time, so long that we believe that if asked when the earliest medium of communication began to exist, I am afraid that no one would be able to answer this question. Communication is the interactive activity of information, and according to communication scholars, "About 100,000 years ago, our ancestors first communicated through nonverbal gestures, and later added the language system to the mix ...... There is abundant evidence that in the late prehistoric phase - -between about 5000 B.C. and 10,000 B.C., both communication activities and communication media had emerged."[57]Denis Schmandt-Bessarat, who specializes in early symbol systems, has demonstrated through archaeological examination that the earliest archaeological material that can prove the use of symbols in the Near East is a Neanderthal dependency from the Middle Paleolithic period, as late as 60,000 to 25,000 BCE.[58]The history of human communication

[56] by James Gleick,Bo Gao, A Brief History of Information, People's Post and Telecommunications Publishing House, 2013, p. 5.
[57] David Crowley, Paul Heyer, The History of Communication -- Technology, Culture and Society, Peking University Press, 2018, 6th edition p. 2
[58] David Crowley, Paul Heyer, History of Communication -- Technology, Culture and Society, Peking University Press, 2018, 6th edition p. 6

is as long as the history of human society. With human beings, there is human communication, and information communications a basic need for human survival and development. Human communication activities have also undergone great changes under the impetus of communication needs and the advancement of productive forces production relations. Summing up what previous generations have said, human history has so far experienced eight representative communication revolutions.

The first was the graphic transmission of primitive frescoes and the use of sound, light and other symbols; the second was the sharing of linguistic information, with precise basic carriers and tools for information communication; the third was the recording of written information, which could preserve information and transcend the limits of space and time; the fourth was the proliferation of printing technology, which allowed for mass reproduction and the transmission of information over long distances, realizing the social communication of information, with newspapers and books as carriers and the modern newspaper as professional social organizations showed soon afterwards. The fifth is radio technology, which allows the transmission of information in real time over long distances, making news and information a happening event, initially forming a space of "presence" for transmission, and bringing about the radio media and radio media; the sixth is television technology, which enables the visualization of information transmission and real-time multimedia transmission over long distances, further realizing the concept of "presence". "The seventh time was the Internet technology, which realized real-time multimedia interaction at a distance, not only "presence", but also "participation". The eighth time is the mobile Internet broadband technology, intelligent, big data, cloud services, providing society with new information communication capabilities, with the characteristics of high efficiency, low cost and fast operation, the development of convergent media has become the goal of all kinds of traditional media and network media.We can see from the above that the first three revolutions are the revolutions of information carriers, and in the middle are three revolutions of transmission methods that gave birth to three traditional media: newspapers, radio and TV, while the last two revolutions formed new media and multimedia, and the information channels are getting more and more open.

The eight information revolutions we can briefly list as follows:

Stage	Name of carrier	Content characteristics	
First information revolution	Original frescoes	graphics	Information Carrier Revolution
SecondI nformation Revolution	Oral Communication	language	
Third Information Revolution	Text Communication	Shareable symbols	
Fourth information revolution	Paper Communication	Reproducible symbols	Transmission method revolution
Fifth Information Revolution	Radio communication	Sounds, symbols	
Sixth Information Revolution	TV communication	Sound and image	
seventh information revolution	The internet	Remote, multimedia	Interaction Capability Revolution
eighth information revolution	Internet mobile	be present	

Figure 1.1

II. Media development re-understanding: from 1G to 5G media iteration

If the eight revolutions of information communication indicate the change of human information activities, then taking professional media as a watershed, human information communication activities can be divided into two major parts, one before the emergence of media, and one after the emergence of media. From the perspective of media development, it can be further divided into three stages. 1.0 is the traditional media stage, including the emergence and development of newspapers, radio and television; 2.0 is the cross-media stage, moving from traditional media to the Internet, and maintaining the one-way communication from the central media to the audience despite the emergence of online media and the expansion of traditional media to online media; 3.0 is the self-media or social media stage, which is a reversible transmission of peer-to-peer, and sharing and linking become the key.

In terms of mobile communication technology, we have seen that almost every iteration from 1G to 5G has brought about a change in the medium. Mobile communication research began in the 1980s, and 1G was launched around 1990 with analog electrical signals, which could only carry out voice transmission and had little impact on traditional media;2G, which began to be studied in the 1990s, became commercially available after the new century, and the analog signal was changed to digital signal, and the data transmission rate reached 32kbps (32 kilobits per second), so that we could read text and spread pictures online, which marked the arrival of the era of "self-media" and entered the "microblogging" era.;Around 2009 3G began to be pushed into society, information transmission from narrowband to broadband mobile, and the data transmission rate reached 2mbps (2 megabits per second), 66 times more than 2G, the network speed is more than 20 times faster, 3G marks the real arrival of the mobile era, people can watch movies on the cell phone, as far as the media, and into the mobile QQ and "WeChat era";Around 2014, 4G became commercially available, with data transmission rates up to 100mbps (100 megabits per second), which is 50 times more than 3G, and the network speed has increased by more than 30 times, and mobile communication has entered the era of primary intelligence, which can be called the "short video era" in terms of media;5G is put into use again around 2019. 5G's 5 distinct features are: high speed, 5G's theoretical data transmission rate up to 10 Gbps (10 gigabits per second), 100 times faster than 4G; ubiquitous network, including extensive coverage and deep coverage connectivity; low latency, the delay between information reaches milliseconds, which is 40 times faster than the speed of sound; low power consumption, the band time is greatly extended; everything smart and reshape the security system, 5G will have more connections and intelligent processing, forming an invisible highway of everything connected, and more media can be exercised on this invisible road.We do not know what kind of biased new media forms will emerge, but there is a saying that 4G changes life and 5G changes society, and it is foreseeable that 5G will change the shape of social communication more and more profoundly.

III. Reflections on the information revolution and media change observation

In his "A Brief History of Information," American scholar James Gleick quotes computer scientist Jaron Lanier as indicating a sense of the information explosion, "It's as if you squatted down and buried a tree seed, only to have it grow so fast that it swallows up the town you live in before you have time to stand up ".[59]In the subtitle of the book, James Gleick uses the term "torrent" to describe the development of information, "information is like a tumbling torrent that overwhelms people".[60]The Chinese financial writer Wu Xiaobo defined the development of the Internet in China as "a volcano that is erupting" in his book "The Biographical of Tencent".[61]Both the "flood" and "volcano" are metaphors for the rapid development of information in this era. Of course, such development is not sudden, but has a history of accumulation, in the above-mentioned development of information communication, we see the following three directions and characteristics are relatively clear.

(i) The speed of information dissemination is accelerating exponentially

Each media period has a significant acceleration compared to the previous one. This acceleration can be derived in our experience and can be

[59] James Gleick in his A Brief History of Information,Bo Gao, People's Post and Telecommunications Publishing House, 2013, p. 388.
[60] James Gleick in his A Brief History of Information, Bo Gao, People's Post and Telecommunications Publishing House, 2013, p. 397.
[61] Wu, Xiaobo, Biography of Tencent: 1998-2016, Evolution of Chinese Internet Companies,Zhejiang University Press, 2017, p. 4.

expressed quantitatively. For example, if the frequency of any information that can be disseminated between receivers or disseminators within a unit is expressed, it is obvious that this acceleration is so obvious from the spoken period to the mobile connected media period. It can be said that this change in the amount of information in a media for the previous media period is exponential. We even have reasons to believe that this accelerating effect of information dissemination is one of the main motives for the change of social values and social culture.

(ii) The amount of content disseminated is increasing exponentially

As with the speed of communication, there is one element that runs through the information Communication that is also becoming extremely large, that is, the amount of content carried by information, specifically the amount of information transmitted between any information recipient or disseminator per unit of time is increasing exponentially. The text, language and image symbols carried by newspapers, radio, television and the Internet are increasing, especially in the network era. We clearly find that the amount of content per unit of time is also moving exponentially with the process of communication revolution.

(iii) Exponential dissipation of linear characteristics of information communication

Information communication has always had a clear linear logic, and this linear logic is determined by the four-dimensional space-time[62] in which we live. For example, if A says, "Raise a glass to invite the moon, and the shadow becomes three", A must conform to the linearity of time when spreading it out, no matter it is expressed in spoken or written words or images, and B must also conform to the linearity of time when receiving it. When B receives it, that is, when he listens to it or reads it, he must also read it according to the linearity prescribed by A. But although when we observe this process "up close", it is obvious that the structure

---

[62] According to the concept of physics, we live in a three-dimensional space composed of "length, width and height", plus a timeline of motion, forming a four-dimensional space-time, the same meaning of the latter

of communication or reception is governed by the time line, that is, the communication process must follow a strict time line, the information attached to this structure is not at all, the information can be unattached to the time line, From the period of spoken language to the period of mobile Internet, the non-linearization of information in the linear structure of time has become more and more obvious, from the communicator's freedom to combine all kinds of information into the communication timeline to the receiver's freedom to combine all kinds of information into the reading timeline, the degree of fragmentation, showing an exponential increase trend.In the communication technology constantly several parts, especially the network communication, intelligent communication, the emergence of cloud technology, let us have another macro level speculation, that is, information (the symbolization of consciousness) itself, can be not dependent on the existence of the timeline, only in the process of communication, only present linear characteristics, if so, information is beyond the limits of four-dimensional space-time.It is an independent unit that exists at least in a fixed dimension of time, and the development of communication technology is the continuous development of the process of dissolving the linear constraints of communication and increasing the independence of information, which is an important factor that we need to pay special attention to after the exponential increase in the speed and content of communication.

PHILOSOPHY OF SCIENCE: A NEW PERSPECTIVE ON UNDERSTANDING COMMUNICATION PRACTICE

As mentioned earlier, communication has always been a discipline carried by time, and the current linear classification of communication research has encountered difficulties in the face of practice, which requires us to find new theoretical paradigms and research perspectives.

I. Philosophy of science has long been the basis for thinking about communication

Examining the past research in communication studies, in general terms, it has never been divorced from its philosophical basis. Of the three major schools of communication ----, the positivist school, the critical school, and the technological school (the media environment school), critical research has been used most often at the level of cultural studies. Critical and cultural studies are mostly based on macro-level "stimulus-response" logic, and in the past the study of information communication was mainly focused on the philosophical "true and false" binary logic of cause and effect. Especially at the cultural study level of communication, most of them are based on philosophical thinking, such as semiotics, structuralism, analytic philosophy, phenomenology, etc., and draw their wisdom from philosophical sages such as Plato, Socrates, Descartes, and Kant. In applied communication and media environment studies, there is also a lot of philosophical thinking about science that relies on natural science, and generally adopts linear causal logic as its basis. It can be said that philosophy has long been the foundation of information communication.

The philosophy of science, as a part of philosophy discipline, has actually entered into the theoretical application of information communication long ago. Now the explanation of philosophy of science on information communication is mainly a continuation of the previous research, which is a new explanation of the new communication based on the progress of natural science, using the philosophical thinking brought by natural science, and this study does not mean that it is a negation of the previous research,but precisely the research progression that is based on previous studies.

Past research can be broadly divided into the following models.

The first is the classical mechanics philosophy represented by determinism and the law of cause and effect, which can be understood as the "Newton + communication" model. Many of the theories in communication that rely on causality and decision as the premise of thinking are based on philosophical thinking triggered by classical mechanics, especially for communication effects, audience research, media research and other communication research that is result-oriented.

The second is the research based on Marxist philosophy, which can be understood as the "Marx + communication" model. The specific expression is the research based on the relationship between economy and society, such as the numerous theories of the critical school.

The third is research based on mathematics, which can be understood as the "mathematics + communication" model, such as the introduction of Shannon's information theory and Wiener's cybernetics, etc.

It should be said that all these studies share a common feature, that is, the combination of causal laws and classical logic, which basically rely on the philosophical logical framework extended by the foundation of natural philosophy.

II. From History to Reality: The Possibility of scientific-philosophical Explanation of Science

(i) From the perspective of the history of science

Both natural sciences and social sciences are branches of rational research in which mankind explores laws. In the long search for truth in the past, the natural sciences and the social sciences have at times drawn on each other.In fact, in ancient times, the study of natural science and social science were not separate. Since the emergence of natural science before social science in modern times, it has continuously injected nutrients into social science, and in turn, social science has also influenced natural science. The combination of the two has also produced very good interdisciplinary results. Lenin pointed out as early as the beginning of the last century that the natural sciences running into the social sciences was an increasingly powerful trend in the 20th century.[63] This is because the natural sciences, which are ahead of the curve, can constantly export new methods and theories to the social sciences and promote the development of the social sciences. For example, the introduction of evolution into the social sciences has produced social evolution, media evolution, etc.; and then the introduction of information science into communication has produced the influential information theory; and the introduction of brain neuroscience into the field of philosophy has created a Damasio monistic system that breaks the dualism between mind and body, etc. So from the perspective of the history of science, the introduction of the philosophy of science into the study of communication is with the construction of a new system of interpretation, not only possible, but also necessary.

(ii) From the nature of information in communication activities

Information itself can be an object of scientific investigation. Whether information is seen as a bit, a symbol, a meaning, or an energy has some validity and is generally accepted in the study of information communication, but all of these concepts can also be used as objects of scientific study. Viewing information as bits or symbols has been shown by Shannon to be not only arithmetical but also applicable; viewing information as a symbolization of consciousness has been shown by Damasio that in fact consciousness has a material basis or is material in nature; viewing information as energy is undoubtedly a concept that is itself examined and arithmetical by the traditional field of physics. So information has scientific verifiability, regardless of the interpretation of information from any known level. Therefore, the concept of "information", which is the core element of communication, has the possibility of being explained by the philosophy of science.

---

[63] See The Complete Works of Lenin, vol. 20, p. 189.

(iii) From the perspective of media technology

From the perspective of media technology, scientific-philosophical explanations are more in line with the characteristics of social media communication. Human society's communication activities through media have taken eight turns: image symbols, language, text, print, radio, television, online media and mobile media, and the ongoing technology based on 5G is the depth of the eighth turn. Each turn has had a profound impact not only on communication itself, but also on the culture, politics and economy of society. The basic driving force of media technology change is to shorten the time of information dissemination, expand the content of communication, and change the space of communication. For the transformation of space-time, the explanation that theoretical physics, especially quantum mechanics, can give is by far the most scientific explanation of the known research results of human society. Therefore, from the perspective of research on media technology, quantum mechanics is a more fundamental theoretical system with explanatory power.

(iv) From the viewpoint of media practice

The difference between social media and traditional media lies in the change of communication elements. We divide the elements of social media communication into the following six points[64]: content, channel, audience, scene, emotion, and relationship. For the explanation of these elements, the perspectives of traditional communication theory and philosophy of science are different. We have broken down the differences between the two as follows:

At the level of content, traditional theory takes the perspective of "the amount of information conveyed by symbols", while philosophy of science takes the perspective of "information entropy". At the channel level, traditional theory takes the perspective of "linear communication", while philosophy of science takes the perspective of "spatio-temporal dimension"; at the audience level, traditional theory takes the perspective of "receptive psychology", while philosophy of science takes the perspective of "multiple universes (such as self-media)". At the scene level, traditional theory takes

---

[64] This section is explained in detail in Chapter 2, Section 3 of this paper.

the perspective of "field theory" in sociology, while philosophy of science takes the perspective of "integral combination of probability elements"; at the emotion level, traditional theory takes the perspective of "probability combination of audience psychological variability", while philosophy of science takes the perspective of "uncertainty"; at the level of relationship, traditional theory takes the perspective of "exact energy conservation", while philosophy of science takes the perspective of "quantum entanglement " as the perspective.

So in terms of media practice, the philosophy of science is able to propose a self-contained set of explanations for the communication practices of social media, but of course this part of the explanation needs to be argued in detail.[65]

III. Paradigm change in the philosophy of science of information communication

Our choice of a philosophy of science perspective to explain social media is not only grounded, but also necessary and plausible, which requires further clarification of the concept of philosophy of science and a discussion of the basis for its introduction into communication science and the possible consequences.

(i) Historical development of the philosophy of science

Arguably, the study of the history of philosophy of science has been relatively short-lived, with a history of just over 20 years. The academic organization "The history of philosophy of science working group" (see: http://www.hopos.org/) began to appear in 1993. But the first international history of philosophy of science conference, held three years later at Virginia Polytechnic Institute and State University, was held from April 19 to 21, 1996. The International Society for the History of Philosophy of Science was formally established at that meeting, marking the emergence of the study of the history of philosophy of science.In 2011, the Journal of the International Society for the History of Philosophy of Science (HOPOS)

---

[65] This section is detailed in Chapter 3 of this paper.

was launched, and thus the history of philosophy of science as an emerging field of research has been institutionalized.[66]

According to the testimony of Professor Anwei Fu, philosophy of science is a symbiotic system of knowledge with science and philosophy. From the perspective of Oeno's history, it is mainly divided into the genealogy of philosophy of science in the ancient Greco-Roman period, the genealogy of philosophy of science in the medieval period, the genealogy of philosophy of science in the modern era, the genealogy of philosophy of science in the analytical era, the genealogy of philosophy of science in the post-modern era, the genealogy of philosophy of science in historicism, etc.

The genealogy of scientific-philosophical thought in the Greco-Roman period served as an exploration and definition of the study of philosophy of science, mainly in terms of atomism, conceptualism, and the four causes. The genealogy of the philosophy of science in the medieval period is characterized by the continuity of the development of ideas between the scientific revolution and the modern era, and the establishment of its holistic philosophy of science, with representative theories such as "Medieval cosmology: discussions on finitude, space-time, emptiness, and the multiplicity of the world. Its representative theories, such as "Medieval Cosmology: A Discussion of Finitude, Space-Time, Void, and the Multiplicity of the World," contain the intellectual genealogy of Neoplatonism: it clearly defines the place of man in it, places the relationship between man and God at the center of moral cultivation, strengthens the alliance between science, philosophy, and religion, and has a stronger mystical dimension. It also contains the Aristotelian genealogy of knowledge and the genealogy of nominalism (Nominalism)"[67]The intellectual genealogy of the development of the modern philosophy of science was mainly triggered by the revolutions in the natural sciences: "the Copernican revolution and Francis Bacon; Descartes' analytic geometry and rational skepticism; the collaboration between Locke and Boyle, Newton-Leibniz-Kant, etc. The intellectual genealogy of empiricism ...... The intellectual genealogy of rationalism ...... The intellectual genealogy

---

[66] An Weifu, Philosophy of Science: A Historical Examination of the Basic Categories,Beijing, Beijing Normal University Press 2015, p. 3

[67] An Weifu, Philosophy of science: a historical examination of the basic categories, Beijing, Beijing Normal University Press 2015, pp.6-8

of mechanism: the philosophical ideas of science of Newton, Leibniz and Kant. Newton's and Leibniz's debates about many scientific issues sparked Kant's critical philosophy."[68]So far it can be seen that the exploration of natural science and the summary of laws began to make the study of philosophy of science to the depth of knowledge.

The modern philosophy of science has several main lines of research: analytical philosophy, postmodern philosophy and historicism. Their main features are to try to absorb the latest scientific research results in large quantities, to materialize and atomize the unit of analysis, and to scientificize the analytical process. Among them, "the philosophy of science in the analytic era has the following three main genealogies: the logical atomism of Russell and others; the logical empiricism of the Vienna School; and the criticism of logical empiricism by Popper and Kuaiin and others."[69]The literature and genealogy of postmodern philosophical thought, "focuses on the ideological distinctions and connections between modernism and postmodernism in the philosophy of science, with an emphasis on research platforms such as historicism, relativism, constructivism, and the resulting 'historical turn' ' practical turn," 'rhetorical turn,' 'cultural turn," and 'social (academic) turn.' "[70]And "The Genealogy of Historicist Knowledge: The Historical Turn as a First Approach to Post-Positivism ......: Toward Scientific Positivism as a Second Approach to Post-Positivism ......: Towards Constructivism as a Post-Positivist Philosophy of Science The third and most recent path of post-positivist philosophy of science. This path emphasizes mainly the decisive importance of the actions of scientists (cognitive and social actions) for scientific activity."[71]

Among these lines of research, analytic philosophy is the philosophical school closest to the natural sciences among them, and among them, logical analysis is closer to the natural sciences than linguistic analysis, so

---

[68] An Weifu, Philosophy of science: a historical examination of the basic categories, Beijing, Beijing Normal University Press 2015, p9

[69] An Weifu, Philosophy of science: a historical examination of the basic categories, Beijing, Beijing Normal University Press 2015, p10

[70] An Weifu, Philosophy of science: a historical examination of the basic categories, Beijing, Beijing Normal University Press 2015, p11

[71] An Weifu, Philosophy of science: a historical examination of the basic categories, Beijing, Beijing Normal University Press 2015, pp.12-13

we cite the following diagram to illustrate the trajectory and main ideas of logical empiricist philosophy.

	Exploration before logical empiricism	The logical empiricist view	Exploration after logical empiricism
Science & Philosophy	Historical evolution of the image of science	Rejecting Metaphysics with Logical Analysis	The conceptual community of science-philosophy
Analysis & Synthesis	Relevance of analysis and synthesis	Analysis-Integrated Dichotomy	An attempt to go beyond the dichotomy
Theory & Observation	Rationalist Attitude	Empirical-reductionist position	Constructivism's path
Discovery & Defense	Evolution of the development model	The Dichotomy of Discovery and Defense	The cycle of personal and public knowledge
Interpretation &Understanding	The Dichotomy of Interpretation and Understanding	The separation of interpretation and understanding	The Rhetorical Turn and its Critique
Normative &Revolutionary	The Course of Scientific Norms	Static analysis of the normative language of science	Integrating Endohistoricism and Exohistoricism
Reality &Construction	Realism and Anti-positivism	Dissolving Positivism with Logical Empiricism	The Integration of Realism and Constructivism
Nature &Culture	The Rise and Fall of Natural Philosophy	Insisting on the demarcation between science and culture	Rethinking the study of science and culture
Knowledge &Society	The Advance and Revolt of Scientism	The extreme form of scientism	Integrating the Study of Science and Technology

Facts &Values	The origin of the idea of facts and values	Dissolving value judgments with factual judgments	Exploration of the Dichotomy between Facts and Values

The above figure is from An Weifu, Philosophy of Science:
A Historical Examination of the Basic Categories Beijing,
Beijing Normal University Press 2015, p. 17
Figure 1.2

(ii) Philosophy of science as a bridge between the natural sciences and the humanities

In the preface to Philosophy of Science: A Historical Examination of the Basic Categories, Professor Anwei Fu once pointed out that "in the most beautiful and profound sense of philosophy, a humanist understanding of science is a philosophical understanding of science".[72] According to Marx's dialectical materialism and historical materialism, matter is the first, perception is the second, all social relations are mediated by things, and these relations are always between man and man and between man and nature. In other words, to talk about the relationship between man and things requires thinking about man from the level of real matter, and to talk about the relationship between man and people, which requires things as intermediaries, or to return to the level of the relationship between man and things and cognition. Marx explained long ago that "industry is the historical relationship between nature and man, and therefore between natural science and man in reality. Thus, if industry is seen as an open demonstration of the essential power of man, then the human nature of nature, or the natural nature of man, is also understandable, so that natural science will lose its abstract material or rather idealistic orientation and will become the basis of the science of man, just as it has now, albeit in an alienated form, become the basis of real human life. "[73]

The period of great development in the knowledge and use of things

---

[72] Wartowski,Conceptual Foundations of Scientific Thought --An Introduction to the Philosophy of Science,Fan Dainian et al.,Seeking Truth Press,1989,Preface
[73] Marx and Engels, The Complete Works of Marx and Engels, vol. 42, People's Publishing House, 1979, p. 128

began when modern science took off with the natural philosophical studies of Newton and others. "Just over two hundred years after Newton, natural philosophy entered a golden age of thought: in Germany alone, Leibniz published the Monadologie in 1714, Kant published the Allgemeine und Theorie des Himmels in 1755, Fichte published Crundlage der gesamten Wissenschaftslehre in 1794, The Science of Knowing in 1804, Schelling's Ideen zu einer Philosophie der Natur in 1797, and Hegel's Natur Philosophie in 1816, etc.That is, Newton's attempt to replace 'natural philosophy' with 'mathematical principles' in his intellectual aspirations instead stimulated the full development of natural philosophy."[74]In this period, science naturally completed its connection with philosophy, and also completed its leadership in the development of the material world, so that the English philosopher Bacon, at the beginning of this period, in his famous book "The New Instrument" published in 1620, uttered the famous words "knowledge is power", which later became the guide of social development. Knowledge is the power to transform the world.

Indeed, science connects not only philosophy to the natural world, but also to the humanities. Numerous scholars, when talking about the role of the philosophy of science, have generally emphasized the bonding role of the philosophy of science. For example, P. Frank, a leading scholar of the Vienna School, in his book The Philosophy of Science, defines the philosophy of science as the link between science and philosophy, as well as the chain between science and the humanities. He says: "The knowledge of science and a systematic approach to tactics and strategy concerning science are the main elements of any philosophy of science".[75]The American scholar Wartowski also argues that "the essence of philosophy of science, as the 'missing link' or 'bridge' between the natural sciences and the humanities, is to interpret the concepts and patterns of scientific thought as objects of humanist understanding, applying the analytical tools of logical criticism and transformation along with the comprehensive effort

---

[74] An Weifu, Philosophy of science: a historical examination of the basic categories, Beijing, Beijing Normal University Press, 2015, p244

[75] Hong Xiaonan et al., The Second Philosophy of Science, Beijing, People's Publishing House, 2009, preface, p. 3

of philosophical generalization to the history of science and contemporary scientific thought."[76]

In identifying the bridging and linking role of the philosophy of science, numerous scholars have also pointed out that the methods of science and the laws of nature can also be a kind of care for social disciplines. s. Toulmin states in the Philosophy of Science: "What the philosophy of science has to deal with is the methodological and epistemological problem, that is, the problem of the ways and means of the researcher's approach to nature", and "Philosophy of science, as a discipline, begins by elucidating the various elements of the process of scientific inquiry: procedures of observation, modes of argument, methods of expression and calculation, metaphysical assumptions, etc., and then evaluates the grounds for their validity from various perspectives: formal logic, practical methodology, and metaphysics. Thus, contemporary philosophy of science is clearly a discipline of analysis and inquiry"[77]Isherick also says: "The meaning of every physical statement exists ultimately in the infinite connection of sensory material that serves as evidence. So isolated sensory material does not interest one here."[78]"Philosophy of science is neither a philosophy purely aimed at science, nor is it all about transforming philosophy with science, but a two-way communication between science and philosophy. From the level of thought, philosophy of science is the transcendence of scientific thought, and this transcendence is the design of the world based on science and the transformation of philosophical outlook, and in turn affects culture in general; from the content of thought, philosophy of science, especially the school of philosophy of science, is nothing but the selection and reorganization between facts and values."[79]

Philosophy of science is not only the application of the laws and

---

[76] Wartowski,Conceptual Foundations of Scientific Thought --An Introduction to the Philosophy of Science,Fan Dainian et al.,Seeking Truth Press,1989,Preface

[77] Toulmin: Philosophy of Science, in Jin Gurun, Selected and Edited: "The View of Nature and Science", Knowledge Press, 1985, pp. 411-412

[78] M.K. Munitz, Wu Muren, Zhang Rulun and Huang Yong, Contemporary Analytical Philosophy, Fudan University Press, 1986, p. 311

[79] An Weifu, Philosophy of science: a historical examination of the basic categories, Beijing, Beijing Normal University Press, 2015, p353

methods of science, but also its bridging role is reflected in the reflection and transcendence of natural science, which is a process of "turning knowledge into wisdom". "Philosophy of science is the reflection and transcendence of natural science, then the difference between different stages or schools of philosophy of science lies in the type of knowledge they rely on and the direction of transcendence of knowledge. In terms of the type of knowledge they rely on, some philosophies of science rely on mathematical sciences such as geometry, algebra, logic, etc., such as Plato, Boethius, Leibniz, Frege, Russell, Wittgenstein, Cain, Lakatos, etc., which makes them often choose the rationalist approach to philosophy of science; some philosophies of science rely on empirical sciences such as biology, physics, chemistry, medicine, etc., such as Aristotle, Darwin,Locke, Beckley, Ayer, Brewer, Flaxen, Collins, etc., which makes them often choose the empiricist approach to philosophy of science; others rely on history of science, sociology of science, and politics of science, such as Kuhn, Feyerabend, Brewer, Setina, Latour, etc., which makes them often choose the historicist or social constructionist approach to philosophy of science. In the direction of going beyond scientific knowledge, in the continuum from factual to value judgments, some take an extreme scientistic position and advocate replacing value judgments with factual ones, such as various Humean, Wittgenstein, Carnap, and other empiricists, especially logical empiricists."[80]

Philosophy of science is a bridge between natural sciences and humanities. Philosophy not only thinks about society through the laws summarized by natural sciences, but also can use scientific methods to study social disciplines, and can think about science from a higher transcendent perspective, bringing ideological impetus to the advancement of science.

---

[80] An Weifu, Philosophy of science: a historical examination of the basic categories, Beijing, Beijing Normal University Press，2015, preface,p5

(iii) A paradigm revolution in the philosophy of science triggered by new communication

The introduction of philosophy of science into communication can be understood as a paradigm revolution in research due to a new communication phenomenon.

Paradigm revolutions are an important assertion made by the famous philosopher of science, Kuhn. According to him, the development of science is one paradigm revolution at a time. The concept of "paradigm" is the core concept of Kuhn's philosophy of science. In his book The Structure of Scientific Revolutions, Kuhn points out that a paradigm has two basic characteristics: first, it is sufficient to "attract an unprecedented number of committed adherents and to divorce them from other competing models of scientific activity. Secondly, it is sufficient to "leave an unlimited number of problems to be solved for a reconstituted group of practitioners. In short, these achievements are both fascinating and imperfect. Any scientific achievement that has these two characteristics can be called a "paradigm". Thus, a paradigm means "some accepted example of actual scientific practice - which includes laws, theories, applications, and instruments together - that provides a model for a particular coherent tradition of scientific research."[81]Although he does not give a coherent, universal definition of paradigm, we can use his description to get a basic idea of what paradigm looks like. Kuhn says: "On the one hand, it (paradigm) represents a whole of beliefs, values, techniques, etc., shared by the members of a given community; on the other hand, it refers to an element of that whole, i.e., specific puzzle solutions: they are used as models and examples that can replace explicit rules as the basis for other puzzle solutions in conventional science. "[82]

Kuhn's "sociological turn" means that the development of scientific thought and theory is not merely an enterprise of scientific rationalism or the application of purely scientific methodology, but a process that incorporates many cultural and socio-historical elements of the scientist.

---

[81] Li Rong, A Study of the Sociological Turn in Kuhn's Philosophy of Science, People's Publishing House, March 2018, 1st edition, p. 88

[82] Thomas Kuhn, Gulun et al, The Structure of Scientific Revolutions, Beijing University Press, 2003, p. 157

Kuhn explores the influence of socio-cultural activities within the scientific community on the growth of scientific knowledge. The hallmark of this sociological turn is that:science shifts from rational cognitive activity to scientific social practice. Scientific socio-practical activity has to have a belief, then the paradigm is this belief;Scientific socio-practical activity has to have a subject, then the subject is the scientific community; conventional science is the period of scientific socio-practical activity; the shift from one conventional science to another conventional science is the scientific revolution.[83]According to Barber, Kuhn brought the theoretical links between the history and sociology of science closer, "leading to a creative revolution in the relationship between the philosophy, history, and sociology of science ...... He drew on concepts and materials from all three professions. "[84]

In fact, the research paradigm of information dissemination is also evolving with the times, and technological changes are forcing the theoretical community to undergo what Kuhn summarizes as a scientific revolution. In fact, philosophical reflections and natural science conclusions are often complementary and mutually influential. The cognition of the philosophy of science chosen in this paper also relies on the conclusions of natural science to unfold, "Natural philosophy is actually the elevation of (some) natural science into a philosophical concept of universal significance, that is, the process of thinking of 'from knowledge to wisdom' "[85]"As soon as the spirit embarks on the path of thought and does not fall into vain, but can maintain the will and courage to pursue the truth, it can immediately discover that only the right method can regulate the mind and guide it to grasp the substance and remain in it."[86]So in this paper, once the thinking of natural sciences is adopted as a basis it becomes clear that the use of philosophy of science as a basis for the explanation of new communication phenomena is a necessity. While most of the traditional communication

---

[83] Li Rong, A Study of the Sociological Turn in Kuhn's Philosophy of Science, People's Publishing House, March 2018, 1st edition, pp.168-169

[84] Barber, Gu Xin et al, Science and Social Order,Sanlian Bookstore, 1991, pp. 9-10
[85] An Weifu, Philosophy of science: a historical examination of the basic categories, Beijing, Beijing Normal University Press, 2015, p274

[86] Hegel, He Lin, ShorterLogic, Beijing, The Commercial Press, 1980, p. 427

explanations rely on causal and deterministic thinking with a typical Newtonian classical mechanics foundation, we find in the study of new communication, especially social media communication, that the main reason for the lack of explanatory power of the current communication theories for new communication phenomena is that they rarely draw from new research ideas from natural sciences. Philosophical thinking based on theories such as relativity, quantum mechanics, string theory, superstring theory, and multiverse are precisely more adapted to the explanation of new communication phenomena.

CHAPTER 2

MEDIA TECHNOLOGY CHANGE AND CONTEMPORARY SOCIAL MEDIA RESEARCH

Media technology is an important driving force for changes in the content, mode and organization of information communication, and according to the media environment school of thought, media technology is even the most important driving force. According to Professor Yu Guoming, "the technological revolution has changed communication practice even more profoundly and dramatically."[87] With the promotion of media technology, contemporary social media present the phenomena of information dissemination and relationship construction, the intermingling of real and virtual time and space, and the coexistence of real and media time dislocation. Specifically, in the era of the Internet-based media technology, social media are different from traditional media such as TV, radio, and newspapers in terms of communication content, communication channels, audience characteristics, emotional participation, transmission-reception relationships, and communication scenarios. Synthesizing the analysis of these characteristics, this chapter analyzes the basic reasons for these changes by explaining media technological changes from a spatio-temporal perspective and applying the philosophical explanation of the concept of dimensionality in quantum mechanics.

---

[87] Guoming Yu, Academic innovation in communication: origin, paradigm and value code -- Presentation at the Roundtable on Rethinking Communication, International Journalism, February 2018

COMMUNICATION BIAS: THE DEVELOPMENT OF GLOBAL SOCIAL MEDIA

I. Definition of social media

According to the British scholar Tom Standage, "A Brief History of Social Media: From Sagebrush to the Internet," the concept of social media has existed since the ancient Greek period, that is, he believes that social media is not unique to the Internet, but is in fact a concept that has always existed, and he believes that social attributes are the underpinnings of media, and that the early human way of information dissemination relied mainly on social networks. Paul Levinson, a master of the media environment school, rejects the term "social media" in New New Media to describe the state of media after the Internet. He also uses the reason that "social media" is not a new concept, and he also believes that social media is a long-standing concept. So if we look at it from a historical perspective, social media is a long-established concept, and we can say that from the ancient Greek period, when "errands" and "oral messages" were used as a means of communication, to the papyrus, and until the printing press was widely used in journalism in modern times, the network of information communication was built on the social network of individuals or organizations. Before the emergence of journalism, the main channel of information communication was "to meet on a horse without a pen or paper, and to send a message to report peace".

It can be said that there are two perspectives of reviewing the communication of information in social media, one is broad, that is, society is viewed as a large media field, which can refer to the communication of information in human social relationships; one is narrow, which is also the general consensus of today's society, which can refer to the information communication activities in social networks composed of the Internet. Since the main purpose of this research paper is to explain the characteristics and laws of socialization of information communication through the development of today's Internet, the definition of social media in this paper adopts a narrow concept, which is the activity of information dissemination through social media networks under the vision of Internet technology as a premise.

Before defining social media, we need to clarify the concept of media. From different perspectives, there are many definitions of media, for example, "The 7th edition of Modern Chinese Dictionary explains 'media' as: 'tools for communication and communication of information, such as newspaper, radio, television, Internet, etc. '. There is indeed an overlap in the meanings of these two words in the dictionary, where the concept of 'media' is limited to the field of media, and its scope is much smaller than that of 'medium', and in this sense, the concept of 'media ' concept is included in 'media'."[88]"'Media' is a new communication institution or form that can express the creator's ideas, developed by new technologies."[89] Some people also define media in both a broad and narrow sense, "'Media', as the name suggests, is the substance that assumes a role in this occurrence of roles and relationships, i.e., the medium or connector. In a broad sense, media is the medium or connector in which all things occur and are connected. In a narrow sense, media in the modern sense, mainly refers to the medium or platform of mass communication, assuming the functions of information planning, organizing, processing, and communication."[90] In the conditions of new media, there are also people who have made a more realistic definition of media, "Media, then, should be the people or organizations that master and operate these media. At this moment, it should be understood more as an individual information publisher."[91] The common denominator of these definitions can be seen in the fact that media is a concept with organizational characteristics. It is generally accepted that media is an institution that reproduces and sends information, and what we call media nowadays mainly refers to TV stations, radio stations, websites, and after the emergence of mobile Internet, also refers to WeChat, Weibo, and many forms of clients. So media is an institution

[88] Wan Ying, Media. Media Concept Discernment,News Watch, 2017.28.024

[89] Wan Ying, Media. Media Concept Discernment,News Watch, 2017.28.024

[90] Ding Zhendong, The essential characteristics and social impact of new media, Journalism and Writing, April 2019

[91] Zhang Bin, Definition of the Concept of "Self-Media" and Considerations, Media Journal, August 2008

that reproduces and communicates information with a commercial or political purpose. Therefore, when we further examine the concept of social media, we will find that social media refers to the organization that relies on the information communication network built by the Internet, and this organization is mainly engaged in information reproduction, editing and communication. Due to the emergence of the concept of "new media", it is now common to divide the media into "traditional media" and "new media". It should be noted that both media concepts are relative in nature, as each new technological change inevitably results in the original dominant media becoming traditional media, while media that emerge from new technologies and are generally accepted will be named new media.

As an independent concept, some scholars believe that the concept of "social media" can be used as "Social Media", however, there is still no uniform definition, and even "Social Media" is still controversial. Social Media" is still controversial whether it is translated as social media or social media or social media. Some scholars believe that "the most distinctive features of social media are its vagueness, rapid innovation and the 'convergence' of various technologies".[92]Some scholars have also examined the concept of social media from the perspective of translation, and the scope of "Social Media" is larger than that of "Social Network Sites", "Social Networking Sites" and "Online Social Networks", and includes the latter.The latter three concepts all include the term "Social Network", which emphasizes the attributes of "interaction" and "social network", but they also have their own different aspects of emphasis.[93]It is believed that the concept of social media comes from Anthony Mayfield's 2007 book "what is social media", which defines social media as a new type of online media that gives users great space to participate. American scholars Andre Kepler and Michael Henlein propose a definition of social media: a series of web applications built on the technology and ideology of Web 2.0, which allows users to produce their own content creation

---

[92] Cao Bolin,Social Media: Concept, Development History, Characteristics and Future--The Ambiguities in the Current Understanding of Social Media, Journal of Hunan Radio and Television University, March 2011

[93] Zhao Yunze, Zhang Jingwen, Xie Wenjing, Yu Jusheng, "Social Media" or "Social Media"? --Translation and analysis of a set of crucial concepts", Journalist, June 2015

and communication.[94]Both domestic and foreign scholars have slightly different definitions of social media, seeking common ground while preserving differences, and if they have anything in common, it is that they both focus on modern media technology as the basis for change, and both rely on or establish social networks as the premise for information communication.

The concept used in this paper is that social media is a vehicle for the communication of information in social networks, an online communication platform in which users participate in spontaneous production and sharing. The reason is twofold. First, according to Standage's examination and Paul Levinson's view, realistically speaking, in a broad sense, social media does have a relatively long history, from ancient Greece to modern times, both the information and the carrier carrying the information are indeed presented based on social relationships in the process of flow. Second, in a narrow sense, the concept of social media is generally recognized in modern society is based on the premise of network technology, so the integration of the two, whether the communication of information to expand the social network, or social networks to make the communication of information more convenient, social media is the carrier of information communication in social networks, including but not limited to microblogs, WeChat, Shake, Douban, Facebook, Youku, Twitter and so on.

II. The Bias of Communication: The Development of Contemporary Global Social Media

The Canadian communication scholar Innes has introduced the concept of "communication bias" in his media studies. In his view, "the medium of communication has a significant impact on the transmission of knowledge in time and space, and it is therefore necessary to study the characteristics of communication with the aim of assessing its impact in

---

[94] Kaplan, Andreas M, Michael Haenlein: Users of the world, unite! The challenges and opportunities of Social Media. Business Horizons (2010) 53 (1) P59-68

cultural contexts".[95]And he argues that in media development there are media that are biased with time and media that are biased with space, citing many examples of oral and ear communication bound by time and eye, written, and written communication bound by space. The nature of the medium of communication tends to produce a bias in civilizations that either favors the idea of time or the idea of space. Moreover, Innis argues that any civilization of different periods has its biased medium, the main tool of communication. The bias of civilization comes from the bias of communication, and the bias of communication comes from the bias of the medium. It can be said that in the age of the Internet, the emergence of social media has changed the spatial and temporal nature of traditional communication, and it can even be said that social media is the "biased" medium of this age.

We say that contemporary social media has become the "biased" media of our time, mainly in terms of its speed of development and influence. Since the United Nations named online media the "fourth media" in 1998, the Internet and social media have been booming, with 600 million computer users and 300 million hosts connected to the Internet worldwide in 2003.In 2008, the global Internet users exceeded 1.6 billion. In 2014, the number of Internet users in the world exceeded 3 billion, and in 2018, the number of Internet users in the world reached 4.4 billion, with the global Internet penetration rate exceeding 50% and 5.1 billion people using cell phones. According to Singapore's "United Morning Post" reported on September 18, 2014, "Internet Live Stats" announced that in 1995, there were only 18,000 websites in the world, in 2004 it reached 50 million.In 2006, it reached 100 million, and in 2014 it even exceeded 1 billion. In 2014, there were 640 million Internet users in China, and in 2018, there were 830 million people, with an Internet penetration rate of nearly 60%.

Since the Internet started to develop in the 1990s, it has gone through three stages: first, the competition of portals before 1995 to 2005, second, the competition of platform and key entrance after 2005, and third, the competition in the field of mobile communication after 2010 when mobile Internet became popular. Or we can also describe it this way, if the characteristics of the Internet is "connect everything", then the late 90s to

---

[95] Hadro Inis, He Daokuan, The Bias of Communication, People's University of China Press, 2003, p. 27

2005 is the connection of content, is the era of Web1.0 and the emergence of online media, after 2005 to the beginning is the connection of people and people, is the era of web2.0 and the rise of social media The current trend is the comprehensive connection of things and things, things and people, and people and people, and it is a new era of intelligence. The influence of social media is also increasing day by day.

III. The main problems encountered in contemporary social media communication research

Much has been written about social media and the dilemmas of social media communication, both domestically and internationally. Overseas, public speeches, articles and books by American communication scholars, scholars at the ICA and many other societies are the main focus. Domestic scholars such as Hu Zhengrong, Yu Guoming, Hu Yiqing, Peng Lan, Liu Hailong, Pan Zhongdang, Huang Dan, Kuang Wenbo and a number of other outstanding scholars have also written extensively.

To sum up the various opinions, scholars still have more worries and confusions about the difficulties encountered in social media communication research. In a reflection on the discipline as a whole, Ji Yan and Yun Guoqiang say, "Compared with many mature disciplines, such as sociology, the basic concepts of communication are confused and lack systematic construction, the theoretical originality is insufficient, and the theoretical discourse is as 'marginalized' as the identity of the marginal disciplines. As a result, communication theory lacks authority and even 'loses its voice'. ...... Berelson even declared in an article that the field was dead in light of the weak academic achievements of mass communication."[96]As far as the studies of Chinese scholars are concerned, some of them are also confused about the present research foundation, such as Professor Shu-Fang Lin of National Chung Cheng University in Taiwan, who argues that firstly, social media research lacks diversity and secondly, three-quarters

---

[96] Chi Yan, Yun Guoqiang, Reflections on the development of communication science and its theoretical poverty, Journal of Henan University (Social Science Edition), vol. 49, no. 2, March 2009

of social media research lacks theoretical foundation.[97]Professor Hu Zhengrong summarizes the research dilemma as too much pursuit of hotspots, which makes the research too scattered and detailed, insufficient systematic training in research methods, and serious depoliticization and neutrality in the value level.[98]According to Professor Liu Hailong, "Chinese communication research has emerged with an obvious instrumental rationality that is light on theory, heavy on application, light on criticism, and heavy on management."[99]Professor Hu Yiqing of Nanjing University argues that the development of the communication discipline establishment has entered a dilemma, while suggesting that in "the current field of communication in China ...... research can start by criticizing the old rigid disciplinary structure."[100]Calling for the delineation of communication boundaries, Hu Yong argues that "Chinese online communication research after 2013 seems to need to start redefining research boundaries, research objects, and reflecting on its own connections and differences with other humanities and social science fields."[101]In his summary of communication education, Chen Tao-wen also mentioned that "some scholars believe that current communication research has the following shortcomings: lack of standardization of research, low level of highly repetitive research, and footnote research in which policy is interpreted."[102]According to Professor Duan Peng, Chinese communication research has been trapped in the 5W logical framework. According to Huang Dan, "Among the many constraints on the development of communication research, the most important thing that needs to be addressed is how to break through the

---

[97] Shu-Fang Lin, Social Media Research-Review and Prospects,Information Society Research, 2017, 32

[98] Hu Zhengrong and Ji Deqiang, Reflection and Transcendence: A Review of Ten Years of Communication Research in China, Journal of Hangzhou Normal University (Social Science Edition), December 2011

[99] Liu, H. L., Localizing Communication Discourse from Audience Research, International Journalism, July 2008

[100] Hu Yiching, The dilemma of the development of communication discipline establishment, Contemporary Communication, April 2011

[101] Hu Yong and Chen Qiuxin, Chinese online communication research: sprouting, burgeoning and starting again, News Front, February2019

[102] Chen Taowen, The development dilemma of Chinese communication research: why and what to do, Journalism University,January 2008

shackles of the functionalist tradition in the framework of thinking."[103]In the face of the current academic dilemma, some propose ways to change, and Professor Yu believes that the way to breakthrough lies in "maintaining a profoundly reflective attitude toward our own academic logic and theoretical achievements."[104]According to Professor Dan Huang, "The present is a great opportunity to re-understand and reconceptualize the field of communication …… needs new resources for imagining new ideas and preventing the use of old knowledge to explain new interactions, thus falling into a cycle of old tunes."[105]It is easy to see that the search for a new explanatory framework has become inevitable by following the footprints of the previous generation of thought.

Faced with the need for paradigm change in the communication discipline, Qionglin Mei, who has devoted himself to the study of the philosophy of science, not only raises questions but also gives his opinion at the philosophical level: "The 'paradigm confusion' in communication is related to the problems and limitations of the paradigm concept itself, as well as to the contextual shift from natural to social sciences . In constructing the conceptual system of paradigm, Kuhn has never made a clear and strict unified definition of "paradigm", which gives it a rich and inexhaustible connotation and leaves a huge space for later imagination and exploration …… it is true that the paradigm concept in the field of communication science faces many difficulties due to its discomfort, but given the openness and great flexibility of the paradigm concept, these difficulties are not absolute and insurmountable."[106]

From the above discussion, we can see that there has been a call for a theoretical dimension in Chinese academia. Communication practice

---

[103] Huang Dan, Transformation from Functionalism to Constructivism, Journalism University February 2008

[104] Guoming Yu, Academic innovation in communication: origin, paradigm and value code -- Presentation at the Roundtable on Rethinking Communication,International Journalism, February 2018

[105] Huang Dan, A Reflection on the Rethinking of Communication Studies,Journalist, December 2014

[106] Mei Qionglin, The Confusion of "Paradigm" in Communication Studies -- Based on the Reflection of the Concept of "Paradigm", Modern Communication, September, 2010

has been leading the theory, and the explanatory power of the theory is relatively insufficient. The main problem boils down to, according to Professors Lin Zhida and Shao Peiren, firstly, the lack of basic theory, secondly, being trapped in the traditional research logic, and thirdly, the urgent emergence of a localized theoretical paradigm transformation.

NEW FEATURES OF CONTEMPORARY SOCIAL MEDIA UNDER THE INFLUENCE OF TECHNOLOGICAL CHANGE

According to American communication scholar Cyrene McCrae, there are three dimensions of mass communication: content, organization and audience. Message content refers to how facts are selected and put together; organization refers to the production and delivery of information; and audience is said to be receptive to the communication message, how people understand the media message. Simply put, this communication analysis includes three dimensions, texts production contexts, reception contexts, and their interrelationships.[107]In other words, these three dimensions can be translated into the three basic elements of media communication: content, channel, and audience. When examining the analysis of communication elements by domestic and foreign scholars, there is a general consensus that content, channel, and audience are the basic elements, although the basic elements of communication are not exactly the same. However, the emergence of social media has reinterpreted the contents of these elements. In terms of audience, because social media communication tends to be timely in terms of feedback from both the transmitter and the receiver, and social networks themselves are a high feedback system, the influence relationship between the transmitter and the receiver has been separated from the traditional media "transmitter-receiver" model, and the participant can also be seen as the audience. In terms of content, the form of information in the social media communication process is composed in various ways, mostly using "language symbols", such as text, sound, images and even VR, the number of information symbols (bits) carrying information is increasing with the development of communication technology, and the form of information symbols is transmitted in the communication process. Both sides are determined in a balanced way. In terms of channels, the channels in social media mainly refer to the media or platforms used for information communication, such

---

[107] Salem McLay,Jingping Zeng, Media power--A sociology introduction, Communication University of China Press, 2007, pp. 3-4.

as WeChat and Weibo, but also include Taobao and Xiaohongshu, which are purely "information selling platforms" relying on social networks, and the producers are almost completely individualized and unorganized. The platforms of information interaction are getting closer and closer to the "refined" decentralized platforms from the "brutal" large platforms in the traditional media period, so the coexistence and even integration of large and small platforms are unique to this matter.

Social media rely on social relationships to build information communication form, and also rely on social relationships to spread information media. In social media, information and human social relationships are a pair of structural relationships, compared to traditional media, the speed of social media information interaction is accelerated, reflecting the digitalization, integration, interaction and networking characteristics[108]of new media, and the communication relationship has also undergone qualitative changes with the uncertainty abated. Internet-based social media information communication makes it faster to generate transmission relationships between strangers, and this kind of communication is included in direct communication and platform communication. The so-called direct communication refers to the ability to establish information communication channels between strangers directly through interactive software such as Facebook and WeChat.Platform communication refers to the ability of individuals to establish interactive relationships with strangers with some meaning through a certain type of platform such as Xiaohongshu and Zhihu. So social media provides a broader range of relationship possibilities and also achieves a broader communication effect, strangers can no longer be strangers, and through this technological advancement a broad connection of transmission and reception relationships is achieved.On the basis of extensive connections, information interaction cultures based on this online relationships such as online communities and group relationships have emerged, so relationships have become another important element of social media communication. After the social media communication in the network society adds the undertones of relationship, two other elements based on the communication relationship emerge, the interaction scene and the

---

[108] Peng Lan, "New media": three clues to the definition of the concept, Journalism and Communication Studies, March 2016

interaction emotion.So on the premise of the change in the transmission-reception relationship, new factors such as relationship, emotion, and scene have been added to the traditional content, channel, and audience. Therefore, in our next examination of the new features of social media, content, channel, audience, emotion, transfer-receiver relationship, and communication scene become the six factors that we need to pay special attention to.

I. Content change: media change affects communication content

In social media, the content changes influenced by media change are mainly reflected in two aspects.

First, the amount of content information is gradually increasing.Since information communication entered the electronic age, the direction of change in media technology is a broader connection, faster interaction, more information volume three characteristics. In the content level, from 2G to 5G can clearly see the change of information communication, from text information to picture information, from image information to VR information. According to communication scholar Peng Lan, intelligent technology entering the content industry shows three characteristics: "First, intelligent-driven content production 2.0, algorithm-based content distribution 2.0, personalization and socialization intertwined, consumption and production of one content consumption 2.0."[109]The evolution of content from text to VR is a change in the amount of information flow, some people believe that the amount of information that images can carry is 3 million times more than text, others believe it is 5 million times, this view has not yet been accurately and credibly measured, but in real life, we can feel the difference in the amount of information is obvious. The amount of information we can get from reading a text message is indeed much smaller than the information we can get from an image. Therefore, with the change of media technology, the trend of communication content from text to image is an objective and observable trend, and the amount of information conveyed also shows an exponential increase.

---

[109] Penland, The New Content Revolution in the Age of Intelligence, International Journalism, June 2018

Second, the content community around the core theme (IP). As information is gradually opened up by media technology through social channels, the content of information communication has emerged with the characteristics of a content community. Once a news, film or event is released, new contents around this theme will appear based on different interpretations.

After 2010, the concept of IP emerged in the film and television industry, around a certain IP theme, a variety of small IP themes will be extended, layer by layer, constantly around a large IP take actions of "interpretation - creation", if the content theme, that is, IP is compared to a star, then the If we compare the content theme, that is, the IP, to a star, then the associated content is like a planet in motion around the star, and the planet can extend its own satellite. Take the case of the spread of the COVID-19 in Wuhan in January 2020 as an example, around this IP (news), there were many different interpretations, including epidemic prevention, government information release, community quarantine, and people's life.

II. Channel change: media changes affect the communication channels

The channels referred to here are the collection of multiple styles of media, including traditional media, self media, websites, platforms, APPs and other channels with information gathering and dispersing ability. In a nutshell, there are two aspects of performance.

First, the change of media technology is positively correlated with the incremental number of communication channels. Facebook active users reaching 2.3 billion in 2019, WeChat active users have reached 1 billion, Twitter 330 million, YouTube active users 1.9 billion, the number of APPs on Android in China is 2.17 million as of 2019, and Apple China regional APPs are over 1.5 million, social has become the mainstream medium. It can be understood that media technology changes promote the increase in the number of mediated, from traditional media to social media over the process, the original large-scale centralized and dispersed information channels or platforms, gradually replaced by decentralized, personalized platform, from the number of this trend will only be more and more, from centralized media to self-media is not so much a personalized platform diversity rather than a kind of information interaction The handover of power.

Second, channel personalization. Since 2007, a variety of social media began to reflect the tendency of personalization, media personalization This is a topic that began with media research, the Chicago School in the United States has conducted early research around this topic, to the social media period, this new change in characterization is plural, rapid, variable three characteristics. It can be said that in the period of traditional media, there were as many traditional media as there were media personalities, but in the period of social media, due to the different team positions and market demands, social media have all gone to the road of personalization. In 2007, Nanfang Weekend also revolutionized its slogan as "Here, read China", and WeChat Public proposed that "even small individuals have their own brands". The slogan of Today's Headline is "Information Creates Value", and various self-media have also created their own iconic character.

It is easy to see that the number of channels for information interaction in the social media era is growing exponentially, and behind this growth is the demand of "audience" for discussion on different topics (IP), or the demand for information communication, and there is even a trend of "human is the terminal".

III. Audience Engagement: Media Change Affects Audience Change

Due to the development of media technology, the media has changed from one-to-many communication to many-to-many communication, point-to-point communication and group communication within groups. The media is changing, and so is the audience.In terms of audience status, the audience has changed from a recipient to a participant, a creator in the self-media era, and a dominant information provider in the "human is the terminal" era.

Audience, as the name implies, is the mass of people who receive information. From the English language, the word "audience" appeared around the Middle Ages, the concept of audience has also undergone a series of changes with the development of the times, and this change is divided into about three periods: first, starting from public speaking more than 2000 years ago, the status of the audience as the recipient was clearly defined as the interlocutor of the public; second, with the development of media technology, the emergence of newspapers, radio and television made the status of the audience characterized singularly: the audience was the receiver, and after being noticed by commercial capital also became a commodity with attention production materials; thirdly, and then the change of Internet technology, the audience changed from the receiver to the participant or even the information publisher. [110]Although some scholars believe that this is still a "transmitter orientation under the guise of audience orientation,"[111]it does not conceal the fact that the status of the audience has increased and its role has changed. From the point of view of the political economy of communication scholars, it is the audience's awakening, and from the point of view of the ability to use information, it is true that with the development of media technology, the audience has gradually acquired more ability and power to use information.

Peng Zengjun believes that the audience in the social media era is: the most familiar stranger. Familiar because in the age of social media, everyone is the audience, and strangers because after the audience has been baptized by social media, everyone is only the information in the communication, no longer three-dimensional.[112]To sum up the past history, it is easy to find that at the audience level, every change in media technology is an increase in the ability to collect and distribute information.Whether it is the audience in traditional media or the "user" in new media, the change of technology is the biggest driving force to change the audience from negative to positive.

Of course, there are those who interpret the relationship between media and audience from a Marxist perspective, where in the practice of social media, seeing is labor and using is producing. The audience becomes a combination of consumption and production, and time is a means of production in the form of interaction in social media. From a Marxist

---

[110] Peng Zengjun, The familiar stranger: audiences in the age of social media, Journalist, November 2016

[111] Ma Feng, The "Audience Orientation" under the guise of "Transmitter Orientation" -- The essence of the concept of "audience as consumer" in the social transition, Journalism and Communication Research, January 2006

[112] Peng Zengjun, The familiar stranger: audiences in the age of social media, Journalist, November 2016

value perspective, the medium becomes a form of private capital, the core of which is the use and appropriation of the audience's time, and the return of capital through the sale of the user's or users' time. So Fuchs argues that labor time is the measure of value production in social media. As with traditional media, the audience's viewing time or

or time spent using the medium is labor time.[113]Facebook, Weibo, WeChat, Twitter, etc. all think of capital value in the same way, and the commoditization of audiences is again evidenced in social media. While this argument has explanatory power, it is a way of thinking about audience from a capital perspective and is outside the scope of this paper, so it will not be examined in greater depth.

IV. Emotional participation: new features brought about by media changes

Regarding emotional involvement, we can recognize it from the following perspectives.

(i) Emotion is a mental tool, following the "imitation-perception" law of brain neuroscience

What is emotion? This is a concept that cannot be fully agreed upon by the broadest general consensus. Some scholars believe that emotions are a natural psychological or even individual spiritual thing that transcends objective existence, while others believe that emotions are a reaction of the organism. Some scholars believe that emotions are a higher function of the human brain, the first psychological tool for human survival and adaptation.[114]According to the American psychologist James, "the perception of events that occur leads to physical changes, and the perception of physical changes is emotion". The American scientist Antonioni Damasio believes that emotion is a kind of mental change produced by receiving external stimuli. I believe that from a scientific

[113] Cai Runfang, Value Production of "Active Audience" -- the controversy of"Audience View" of Communication Political Economy and the "Audience Labor Theory" of Web 2.0,International Journalism, March 2018

[114] Ma Q. X., and Guo D. J., Advances in the study of emotional brain mechanisms,Advances in Psychological Science, November 2003

point of view, Damasio's view is more convincing, whether from the point of view of argumentation or the general recognition of brain neuroscience and philosophy of science, so the concept of emotion used in this paper is derived from the conclusions of brain neuroscience such as Damasio.

There are two accounts of how emotions arise. One is the dualism of mind and body, represented by Descartes and others, to the effect that consciousness exists independently of the body or the objective world, and that emotions originate from consciousness, ontologically speaking, as an independent existence; the other is the understanding of recent brain neuroscience, according to the summary of the famous American brain neuroscientist Antonioni, emotions are an objective reflection of external stimuli and a comprehensive tool for coping with the survival environment. According to Papez, "the proposed emotional circuitry includes the hypothalamus, anterior thalamic nucleus, hippocampus and cingulate cortex". It is generally accepted in modern brain neuroscience that consciousness is derived from objective stimuli and does not exist independently. The second view is generally accepted in the psychology, brain neuroscience, and philosophy communities. In the author's opinion, the second view is more convincing for understanding consciousness and emotions.

It is worth noting that the Frenchman Le Pen has made a widely spread group description of group psychology or group emotion: the rabble. In the study of psychology, there is a more explanatory theory about the generation of group emotions, the emotion rendering theory. The emotion rendering theory believes that human beings will unconsciously imitate others' actions, words, sounds and other external expressions to feel others' emotions, and will also generate cognitive processes through imitation and felt emotions, thus regulating self-cognition. According to the explanation of emotion rendering theory, there is imitation when there is interaction, and there is rendering when there is imitation. Although the psychological and neuroscientific communities differ in their understanding of imitation mechanisms and the regions and structures of the stimulated brain, there is a high level of consensus on the macro-process of "imitation-perception".

(ii) In social media, emotion is already one of the important communication elements

In 2016 the Oxford Dictionary released the term "post-truth". The Oxford Dictionary explains it as "a statement of objective facts that is often less likely to influence public opinion than appeals to emotion and inflammatory beliefs." The New York Times defines it as "a situation in which emotions and personal beliefs are more likely to influence public opinion than objective facts"[115]Some media professionals have also made a more common explanation, saying that "there are too many emotions and not enough facts". According to Zhang Qingyuan and others, in the new media context, the facts in "post-truth" refer to the normative consensus and value consensus that jointly construct the truth. The factual fragments call for both facts and "truths" that are emotionally coerced away from the facts. The "truth" triggers or constructs a broader value, and the value drives the emotion, which further collages the truth based on new factual fragments or imagination of factual fragments, thus constituting a complete development process of post-truth.[116]

From an ontological point of view, what we call truth is always the reproduced "truth" that has undergone a certain structural or procedural treatment. From a historical point of view, facts or truths, are expressed in speech, and media is an important carrier of speech. From the facts of speech in the ancient Greek period, to the facts of speech in the traditional media period, to the facts brought by social media due to interaction, we can clearly see a transformation from one-way facts of speech to interactive facts of speech. The facts of interactive speech are the facts in social media, not necessarily all of them are true, but because of interaction, the number of speakers becomes more, the frequency of interaction is accelerated, and the personal emotions of the speakers are mixed in, making the facts

---

[115] Zhang Qingyuan，Cheng Wenqing, Returning to the fact-value dichotomy: Rethinking post-truth and its rationale in the age of self-media,Journal of Journalism and Communication Studies,September 2018

[116] Zhang Qingyuan，Cheng Wenqing, Returning to the fact-value dichotomy: Rethinking post-truth and its rationale in the age of self-media,Journal of Journalism and Communication Studies,September 2018

become a carrier of emotions, and every fact interacted in social media is an expression of emotions. As Yu et al. found, "In the "post-truth" context, emotionally expressed news texts are more likely to activate cortical activity and attract audiences to read them, which also explains the phenomenon that emotionally expressed texts are more likely to spread in the channel."[117]

From a philosophical point of view, truth, post-truth, and emotion are also philosophical propositions, the core of which involves the philosophical reflection on "facts and values". The philosopher Hume argued that "what is true" cannot be derived from "what ought to be true", claiming that reason is only at the service of emotion and that "reason has no influence on our passions and actions". Kant further states that the Humean problem can be understood as a "problem of cause and effect". Kant believes that "value" is a being above "fact", that "value" is an entity beyond feeling, that "fact "can only be produced by "value". So we can see clearly from the philosophical point of view that facts cannot exist independently in the environment of communication, as long as in the process of communication, facts are the carriers of values, that is, facts in communication are just a way of speech of emotions.

Zhu Xingping of Central University of Finance and Economics and Zhang Wei of Xiamen University found the same in their research on facts and emotions. They studied the 15 news events with the highest attention heat in WeChat in 2017 and concluded that the expression framework of WeChat pop-up articles includes: specialization, originality, emotional headlines, content and origin from the Internet, and the combination of graphic and textual content forms commonly. From this, it was deduced that more than 60% of the explosive articles were heavily emotional, with obvious emotionalization of political and social events and strong agitation.[118]Tang Xuemei pointed out in her research on emotions and social media that "emotion is a kind of short-lived, high-intensity, sudden physiological reaction mainly influenced by external events, often expressed

---

[117] Yu Guoming, Qian Feifan, Chen Yao, Xiu Lichao, Yang Ya, The mechanism of "post-truth": the communication effect of emotional texts, Journal of Xi'an Jiaotong University (Social Science Edition), July 2019
[118] Zhu Xingping and Zhang Wei, The Emotional Expression of WeChat Explosive Articles and the Public Opinion Communication of Hot Public Events,China Publishing, January 2019

through expressions, body movements or language, and is a basic human psychological activity, and the vast majority of social media information belongs to user-produced content, and social media information communication is essentially interactive communication between users, and the expression of emotions in interpersonal communication is a common phenomenon."[119]

In January 2020, domestic and international events occurred frequently, such as the assassination of a senior general of the Iranian army in the United States, the new movement of the yellow vest movement in France, the new move of the UK to leave the European Union, the COVID-19 outbreak in China, etc. All kinds of related information were widely spread on WeChat's circle of friends, microblogs, and various clients of traditional media, and a lot of the untrue information is more about emotional communication.Research has found that rumors, a specific form of speech that relies on emotions, become prevalent whenever a major social event occurs.According to the 2015 New Media Blue Book, "the average media interception of rumors in WeChat is 2.1 million times,"[120]which is always accompanied by rumors, Even though the government and scholars have called for not spreading rumors, not believing rumors, and not creating rumors, it is difficult to ignore such highly emotional information. And in the past practice of social media communication, it is not difficult to find that a large number of information that is retweeted and commented on almost always has personal emotions in it. In social media research, many of them are characterized by "writing is opinion, communication is attitude".

Therefore, as a communication researcher, the psychological element of "emotion" should be included in the objective examination of social media, whether from a philosophical, theoretical or practical point of view, as it is already one of the important elements of communication.

---

[119] Tang Xuemei, A theoretical review of social media research on emotional information dissemination, Modern Intelligence, March 2019

[120] Liu Xin, WeChat intercepts rumors 2.1 million times a day,Beijing Daily, June 25, 2015,the 13th edition

(iii) Imitation and perception in social media under emotional infection theory

According to our philosopher Zhao Tingyang, "what consciousness has is what the world has", whose thinking points to the fact that people build the world we speak of through their thoughts. In the communication practice of social media, it is not difficult to find that information wrapped with emotions is most likely to be widely spread. These messages often stimulate the audience's emotions through words, pictures, images, etc. The audience is essentially an act of imitation when forwarding these messages, and in the process of creating them again, they are also intentionally or unintentionally imitating the emotions of the received messages. Subsequently, a unique set of value judgments is formed, and according to these value judgments, an "information cocoon" is formed. Zhang Qingyuan et al. argue that in the new media era, there are two aspects that cannot be ignored: (1) emotions are driven by values, that is to say, the truth under the hostage of emotions constructs values, and these values influence the truth through emotions;(2) When selected fragments of facts are collaged together with emotions to hold the truth hostage, the clear causal link from fact to truth is subverted and the truth is no longer a proven fact, but information that fits some emotion that people are willing to choose to believe or pretend to believe.[121]Of course, this process is structural and complex, and it is not the intention of this paper to explicitly argue for the generation of a "value-like ecology", but it is possible to conclude that social media itself is an imitation process of emotional infection. Many scholars share the same view, such as Kramer, who points out that in Facebook comments, emotional messages can influence the audience's emotions by means of emotional contagion.[122]Yu GuoMing et al. also argue that "emotional information can influence the audience's perception of information content by means of emotional

---

[121] Zhang Qingyuan,Cheng Wenqing, Returning to the fact-value dichotomy: Rethinking post-truth and its rationale in the age of self-media,Journal of Journalism and Communication Studies, September 2018

[122] Kramer.L.L. Learning emotional understanding and emotion regulation through sibling interaction 【J】.Early Education and Development,2014,25(2):160-184.

infection."[123]Emotion is an organized, deeply embedded, and constantly changing state of mind. People can perceive changes in the emotions of others by capturing the emotions of others, and this interaction process is called emotion contagion. Current theoretical hypotheses on the formation mechanism of emotion infection include imitation-feedback mechanism, association-learning mechanism, language-modulated association mechanism, cognitive mechanism, and direct induction mechanism, among which the imitation-feedback mechanism is accepted by most scholars[124].Emotion infection theory is explained from brain neuroscience that imitates actions first and then generates explanations, which means imitating others' actions first and generating characteristic emotions through imitating others' actions, which is also generally supported by contemporary famous brain neuroscientists such as Antonioni and Gazzaniga. It can be seen that emotions are the product of perception before generation, and social media, due to frequent interactions, can easily perceive each other's emotions through text, pictures, images and interactive information and imitate and generate personal retransmission of emotions.

V. Relationship first: the new characteristics of communication brought by media change

The relationship between the transmitter and the receiver of information is the relationship between the transmitter and the receiver of information, and the relationship has changed from "strong relationship" to "weak relationship",and then to "strong relationship" again in different media periods. From the magic bullet theory at the beginning of the 20th century to the return of the powerful effect theory in the 1970s, the recipient-receiver relationship has been continuously recognized, but it is undeniable that they all have a mutual influence on each other.

---

[123] Yu Guoming, Qian Feifan, Chen Yao, Xiu Lichao, Yang Ya, The mechanism of "post-truth": the communication effect of emotional texts, Journal of Xi'an Jiaotong University (Social Science Edition), July 2019

[124] Wang Xiao, Li Wenzhong, and Du Jiangang, A Review of Research on Emotional Infection Theory, Advances in Psychological Science, August 2010

H.C. Ting considers the transmission-reception relationship as a co-evolutionary relationship.[125]From the perspective of information communication, Yumei Dai believes that "1. information communication spreads from the center to the edge; 2. synchronous interactive communication is presented; 3. the era of user orientation comes; 4. other nodes are aggregated with the user as the center. The advantage of communication is the "weak connection" between nodes and the "circle" communication of information."[126]From the perspective of social media, some scholars believe that the relationship between transmitters and recipients is not diffuse, but has a hierarchical similarity between transmitters and audiences, forming a kind of convergent and convergent "flow circle of influence". More specifically, the level of influence and status of the communicator on the network is closely related to the level of influence of the audience it attracts; at the same time, the audience is also more inclined to provide information and communication feedback to the communicator level with similar influence, forming an effective communication channel.[127]

From a political economy perspective, Smets, an audience researcher of the political economy of communication school, argues that media is a production field composed of specific production relations, and the media users are the laborers in the media production field. In social media, the audience changes from passive, to active, to become an active audience, a true producer of meaning.[128]Daily life is integrated into informational capitalism by media technology, and digital media users are involved in

[125] Ding Hanqing, Reconstructing the Relationship between Communicators and Recipients in Mass Communication: An Ecological Perspective on the Relationship between Communication and Recipients, Modern Communication, May 2003
[126] Dai Yumei, A Communication Interpretation of Self-Media, Journalism and Communication Research, May 2011
[127] Xu Xiang, The "circle of influence" effect in social media communication: A media sample-based current affairs mining and analysis, Journal of Social Sciences, Tongji University, March 2017
[128] Cai Runfang, Value Production of "Active Audience" -- the controversy of"Audience View" of Communication Political Economy and the "Audience Labor Theory" of Web 2.0,International Journalism, March 2018

the digital media value chain, serving multiple segments of production, consumption and markets.[129]

Collectively, the phenomenon we can observe in the study is that the transmitter-receiver relationship affected by the change of media technology has brought about new characteristics of communication. First, the transmitter-receiver relationship has changed from a weak relationship to a strong relationship, for example, the feedback between the transmitter and the receiver in the traditional media period needed to go through a relatively long and complicated process, while in the social media period, the process became timely and efficient; second, it has developed from conveying information to negotiating information, for example, from one-way communication in the traditional media period to timely interaction now, social media unifies publishers and receivers into an integrated state of negotiation.Finally, from relatively static information dissemination to dynamic information dissemination, in the traditional media period, our practice and theory are based on static coverage of events, but in the social media period, a news has been a world away from a news in the past, all news are dynamic interpretation after the generation of static appearance.For example, in the "COVID-19 " that broke out in January 2020, the news constituted a kind of "thematic ecology" that unfolded with the combination of time clues, event clues, emotional clues and value clues. The main reason behind this kind of communication ecology, which follows different logics and even intertwines different logics, is the expansion and complexity of information relations, and the expansion of information relations brought about by timely information interaction, which inevitably generates new characteristics based on the speed of communication.

---

[129] Cai Runfang, Value Production of "Active Audience" -- the controversy of"Audience View" of Communication Political Economy and the "Audience Labor Theory" of Web 2.0,International Journalism, March 2018

VI. Scenario-based communication: the new characteristics of communication brought about by media changes

"Scenario-based" is also a new feature of social media communication. As we can see through practice, in social media communication, the transmission-reception relationship forms a common relationship of sharing information, and as practice progresses, this transmission-reception relationship constitutes a sense of ritual, and can form a unique virtual information field unique "niche culture". McLuhan once said that "the medium is an extension of man", and the communication relationship characterized by scenes formed by people in the process of information interaction is the intersection of the extension of man, and the field formed by this intersection constitutes the soil for new information generation, "Scene is information" can also be seen as an extension of McLuhan's "media is information". "Scene" can be understood from the following aspects.

(1) Field is a kind of co-present information sharing. Due to the change of communication technology, the concept of field has been liberated from the face-to-face environment like cinema and party, and social media has built a new type of information field. Dennis McGuire was one of the first scholars to propose the concept of "presence". His research argues that film can "recreate the reception of early audience locatedness ...... millions of ordinary people sharing the same mediated emotional and learning experiences." Although McGuire does not distinguish the specific concept, structure and characteristics of the "field," he clearly suggests the existence of the "field" as a group structure.[130] In the field of information communication, Merovitz has also borrowed Goffman's drama theory to describe the new space constituted by the new media, which actually points out the relationship between the new digital field and the real space. According to Chinese scholar Guo Jianbin, "presence" refers to a "structured" existence and symbolic meaning of media space-time constructed by a specific mass communication system

---

[130] Dennis McGuire, Liu Yannan and Li Ying, Audience Research, Renmin University of China Press, 2006, P.6

and corresponding communication practices.[131]He believes that presence has three characteristics: first, "presence" is a specific medium of time and space; second, "presence has structural characteristics"; third, "presence" is a ritualized scene existence.[132]He clarifies the basis of scene communication to the level of media space-time, which is scientific, and the structure refers to the way information operates and is composed in media space-time. From this, "field" is a ritualistic information sharing unit with independent structure based on spatio-temporal characteristics. In social media, this sense of ritual is determined by a certain theme.That's why social media is full of "carnival" style rituals based on various themes.

(2) Fields are systems of relations. Bourdieu believes that fields are systems of relations, and that these systems of relations are independent of the groups of people identified by these relations. For example, when I talk about the field of a group or an event, I know very well that in this field I will find many "particles" (let's pretend for a moment that we are exploring a physical field) that are subject to various forces of attraction, repulsion, and so on, just like in a magnetic field. Knowing this, once I speak of a field (domain), my attention will be focused on the fundamental role of this system of objective relations, rather than on the particles themselves. We can also follow the formula of a famous German physicist and point out that the individual, like the electron, is a product of the field (domain): in a sense, he is a product of the action of the field.[133]Therefore, from a sociological perspective, a "field" is a relational construct, and the structure of a "situation" consists of the following elements: (a) a spatio-temporal boundary (usually with symbolic or physical signs) formed around the interaction fragment; (b) the co-presence of actors, which allows them to observe each other's complex facial expressions, body postures, language, and other communication media; (c) the awareness of these phenomena

[131] Guo Jianbin, "Presence": Mobile Cinema and Social Construction in Contemporary China, Shanghai Jiaotong University Press, 2019, P.2
[132] Guo Jianbin, "Presence": a media anthropology concept based on the Chinese experience, Journalism and Communication Studies, November 2019
[133] Pierre Bourdieu, [US] Hua Kant, Introduction to Reflective Sociology, Central Compilation Press, February 1998,p. 1145

and the ability to use them reflexively to influence or control the flow of interaction.[134]

(3) Social media constitutes not only a sense of ritual, but also a virtual narrative world and a field of digital existence. Contemporary social media has transformed the boring information communication into an imaginative spatio-temporal saga. It has created a communication scene that deconstructs time into a human-centered one. This spatio-temporal scene not only breaks through the linear limit of time, but also expands the space of human existence and digital communication space.

In the real life space, "field" is a collection of entities, which is the structure of human in the four-dimensional space-time. When the information created by human, or the extension of human consciousness, is separated from the four-dimensional space-time, what is constructed is a digital "field" beyond the four-dimensional space-time, which is not limited by the four-dimensional space-time. The digital scene and the real scene are still in a state of crossover, but with the development of media technology, this crossover will tend to become independent, each with its own boundaries, forming an independent digital scene.

---

[134] Anthony Giddens, The Composition of Society, Life - Reading - New Knowledge,Sanlian Bookstore,May 1998,pp. 409 - 410

SPEED AND DIMENSIONAL CHANGE OF COMMUNICATION IS THE BASIC LAW OF MEDIA TECHNOLOGY CHANGE

When we talked about thinking about media change in the chapter 1, we had pointed out that the change of speed, content, and dimensionality of media communication is the trend of media development, and this phenomenon becomes more obvious in the contemporary social media era and needs further study, and this paper argues that the basic driving force of media development and change is the acceleration of the speed of information dissemination based on the perspective of communication dimensionality.

I. Positive correlation between media technology change and communication speed

(i) The "information world" is accelerating

Looking back at the history of media development in the age of Internet-based media - social media, it is clear that our world is being accelerated by media as the amount of interactable information increases, and that social perceptions are changing based on this acceleration. Three fundamental questions then need to be answered: Can acceleration be measured and on what basis? Why is it that every prediction of media change does not see it as it really is, and every presentation is astonishing? What are the social reasons for the change in social attitudes?

The real change of information communication in society has two dimensions, one is the change of degree of information dissemination carried out in the original dimension, that is, the increase of quantity and the improvement of quality. For example, from the communication of text and pictures as the main symbol carrier to the communication of images as the main symbol carrier, from a single form of information presentation to the communication of integrated information forms, reflecting the increase in the quantity of information dissemination per unit of time, and then for example, the conversion of video dissemination platforms from

Youku, Akiyip, etc. to platforms such as TikTok and Volcano reflecting the acceleration of platforms after decentralization and personalization, and then for example, WeChat and Facebook and other timely interaction software optimization time and time again, public review and yelp and other platforms appear chat function, reflecting the small advance of information interaction acceleration, so, in the original dimension of information interaction acceleration never stop proceeding.

The second is the migration of information communication in dimensionality, that is, turning the contingency of the previous media period into inevitability. For example, the recent case of Alpha GO challenging various Go masters and winning, reflects not only the advantage of artificial intelligence, but also the more abstract recognition of the overwhelming victory of inevitability over chance. If it corresponds to social media communication, we look at it from the perspective of two levels of degree and dimensionality, just like in Go, the improvement of the same dimension is the change of degree, no matter what kind of master you are and how long you practice hard, in The comparison with human opponents can also be understood as a comparison of the degree of information interaction within the limited time and energy. But from the dimensional point of view, what Alpha GO does is high-speed information exchange and processing, and its information processing of Go far exceeds the information processing ability of human, that is, Alpha GO breaks through the amount of information interaction that human understands, and calculates all the chance that human faces as inevitable, surpassing the dimension of human in this game, and striking a descending blow to human. So no matter how good a chess player is, there is no room to fight back in front of the dimensional strike, to borrow a phrase from the novel "Three Bodies" is: destroy you, what does it matter to you.

Therefore, the information communication exponential migration, bring the degree of change, while the accumulation of quantity reaches the threshold, bring the dimensional migration, and enter the next media period. The observation and study of information interaction reveals the fact that the speed and quantity of information dissemination can lead to a qualitative change, which can be understood as a dimensional change, and the abstract conclusion is that inevitability annihilates chance.

(ii) Media technology iteration and information dissemination data volume

Hu Yong believes that "communication in the Internet era is characterized by intermediation, and social media is the large technical intermediary that we favor, and an important issue around social media is communication overload."[135]In order to make the information communication acceleration process more intuitive, the author uses a mathematical representation - the information communication index (not as a basis for calculation, but currently only as a visualization standard) is a measurable basis. Assuming that the initial human social exchange of information is "2", each technological change enhances the amount of information interaction once, and because each technological change is to enhance the speed and amount of information interaction, so expressed in square, so that a symbolic formula can be derived: "the amount of social information interaction = square of information interaction". According to this model, the information interaction in the dimensional view can be reduced to the N2 index. The exponential migration, in the same dimension, reflects the change of degree, such as the optimization of the media, etc. Once the information interaction appears to increase exponentially, the dimensional migration will occur and exceed our expectations. A simple analogy is shown in the figure below.

Information Interaction Index	Media Period
$2^2=4$	Oral Communication
$(2^2)^2=16$	Paper Communication
$【(2^2)^2】^2=256$	Electronic communication (radio and television)
$\{【(2^2)^2】^2\}^2=65536$	Social media period

Figure2.1

---

[135] Hu Yong, In the age of overload, more should be said about the quality of communication,News Front, March 2019

It is conceivable that in the transition from the Internet period to the next media period, the index will increase again to 4294967296. This is an unimaginable dimensional change, as was the case in the previous media dimensional increases, and it has resulted in unimaginable changes in social perceptions and ideas. In the Internet-based media era, for example, the increased speed of information interaction has turned life into a "fast-forward movie", and the ability to disseminate information without barriers has accelerated the change of the world, with a million possibilities in a single moment, because the channels of information production and transmission have been opened up.

In fact, we are already experiencing a vast, all-encompassing and ever-changing world of information. In the information age, metaphors such as "volcanic eruption", "information flood" and "data flood" have been used to illustrate the explosion of information. In 2007, 1.9 ZB of information was sent. This figure is equivalent to 174 newspapers read per person per day worldwide. By 2010, the number of videos available on Youku also exceeded one billion per day.[136] It has been claimed that the arrival of the information society has seen a net increase in computer data of 66% per year, more than 10 times that of other manufactured goods, and that this explosion has wrapped the entire planet in an increasingly dense interconnected network of knowledge and information.[137]According to the IDC Digital Universe study, the amount of new and copied information worldwide in 2020 will be 12 times greater than in 2012, exceeding 40 ZB. We are already in a sea of information.

II. The spatial and temporal dimensions of communication of media technological change explained

In real life, time is not adjustable, while in the social media space based on online media, time can move forward, backward, or even exist without relying on the linear flow of time in the communication of information. Therefore, it is necessary to add the discussion of media time

---

[136] James Gleick, Bo Gao, A Brief History of Information,People's Post and Telecommunications Publishing House, 2013, p. 389.
[137] Kevin Kelly, Xiong Xiang, What Does Science Want?,CITIC Press, 2011, p. 69

to the media space. In this regard, Chinese scholars Shao Peiren[138]and Bian Donglei[139]have done special studies on media time, and Professor Yu Guoming[140]has done studies on media dimension, and these research results are valuable and worthy of our attention and reference.In summary, the worldview of the 20th century differs from that of the 19th century in the following ways: necessary and contingent, deterministic and non-deterministic, information and matter (energy), system and set, historical and logical, artificial and natural, vital and physical, probabilistic and mathematical methods of analysis, created and naturally occurring, emergent and slow, self-acting and self-contained, holistic and local.[141]These changes are associated with scientific and technological developments. Technological changes do not only contribute to changes in results and worldviews, technology is also a decisive condition for change. The change in the effectiveness of media communication from chance to necessity, from decision to probability, from information to matter, technology becomes the means at the operational level and the condition for change in the discipline of communication.

From the point of view of numerical symbolism, there is a certain rule of media change: the number of information communication is increased by an exponential standard (N2) (Figure 2.1 above) to complete the information communication change. The dimensionality in mathematics is simply understood as the addition of a vertical vector to an existing dimension, and each vertical vector is understood as a "real presence" in sociological perception.For example, 0 dimension is a point, increase the vertical is a line, 1 dimension is a line, increase a vertical is two mutually perpendicular lines, composed of two-dimensional plane, three-dimensional is to increase a vertical surface on the plane, composed of

---

[138] Shao Peiren, Huang Qing, Media Time Theory -- A Study for Media Time Concept, Contemporary Communication, May 2009

[139] Bian Donglei and Zhang Xiying, The Coming of Media Time: A Study of the Origin, Formation and Characteristics of the Concept of Time Shaped by Communication Media, Journalism and Communication Research, January 2006

[140] Yu Guoming, The Internet is a "high-dimensional" medium--A discussion of "platform media" as the mainstream mode of future media development, Journalism and Writing, February 2015

[141] Chen Weixing, The Idea of Communication, People's Publishing House, 2008, p. 15

three-dimensional graphics (this is mathematical vector thinking, do not consider increasing the obtuse acute angle is also a cube, that is also to increase the absolute vertical based on the changes that occur), four-dimensional is to increase a vertical vector on the basis of three-dimensional, increasing the absolute presence of time.Because time is the same objective existence as length, width and height in this dimension, the fourth dimension is characterized by a non-linear flow of time. In other words, there is no antecedent cause that leads to a consequence, and the "disappearance of causality" can be understood as the inevitability of chance. For example, buying a lottery ticket is accidental in three dimensions, but in four dimensions it is inevitable, because the result exists objectively. The biggest result of the Internet is the "four-dimensional existence of information". For example, Gaode Map has turned the original uncertain road conditions into certainty.So the fundamental paradox of this media age: three-dimensional people, through a two-dimensional (linear) way of thinking, create four-dimensional products, and we have to read information in a three-dimensional way (linear). The change of media dimensions: ascending dimensions are inevitability annihilating chance, and descending strikes are chance annihilated by the use of inevitable laws in high latitudes. These dimensional changes are also essential factors in our understanding of social media.

CHAPTER 3

PHILOSOPHY OF SCIENCE EXPLAINS THE NEW FEATURES OF SOCIAL MEDIA COMMUNICATION

Contemporary social media information communication can be called "new communication", characterized by huge volume, all-embracing and fast-changing. There are many names for this, such as "cloud news", "flow news", "netflix news", "convergence news "etc. Its performance is that there are many channels of communication, many subjects, many topics and changeable, blurred boundary of communication, convergence of communication, and overall occupying long social time. As mentioned earlier, in terms of specific information communication elements, the new communication has added the elements of relationship, emotion and scene to the traditional elements of content, channel and audience, forming the six elements of communication.In the relationship element, it refers to the transformation from a weak relationship to a strong relationship, or a strong relationship to a weak relationship; the emotional element refers to the convergence or the same of emotions, values, ideas, care perspectives and constant changes; the scene element is the entrance, presence and departure, referring to the here and now and this situation. The traditional in the three elements are also changing, the change in the content element is reflected in the choice of diversity, depth reduction and the prevalence of popular discourse; the change in the channel element is reflected in the interactivity and diversity in the integration of penetration and platform; the change in the audience element is becoming an active audience that teaches reciprocal interaction.The key to the "new communication" phenomenon in social media is the high matching of content, channel, environment, relationship and emotion with the transmitter, forming the largest convention. There are three explanations for the new communication: one is the philosophy of structuralism, the world is open, only partially ordered, and cannot be summarized and does not need to be summarized; the second is the philosophy of technology, using relativity and quantum mechanics, using the presence and absence of the communication subject, quantum superposition of information, quantum entanglement, quantum interference, quantum attraction to explain; the third is the so-called "supramarginal choice" of economics ".It is not the separation of production and consumption, but the unification of the two.Therefore, the equilibrium of information is not the result of product selection, but the result of choosing facts from professional or division of labor, or from relationship and emotion, information is jumping and cross-border, information is more with emotional color.[142]In this paper, a scientific-philosophical explanation of social media is mainly used.

It is important to emphasize that the analytical theories used in this paper for social media communication are derived from the philosophy of science, rather than directly using natural science findings, and are philosophical reflections, explanations and theories following philosophical reflection through the findings of natural science. The philosophy of science based on the use of natural sciences has the following aspects, including the concepts of information entropy, spatio-temporal dimension, multiple dimensions of consciousness, uncertainty, transcendence and quantum correlation, etc. used from the natural sciences of brain neuroscience, relativity, quantum mechanics and string theory, etc.

---

[142] Liu Xiaoying, New forms of journalism and supramarginal choices,Young Journalist, March 2018

CONTENT LEVEL:
INFORMATION ENTROPY

I. "Information is information"

According to the definition in this paper, a message is a symbol of consciousness. The information communicated in social media is an indeterminate thing formed by consciousness. We have found in our past research that many scholars have given rich and in-depth explanations for the understanding of information from different disciplinary perspectives, among which the more representative definitions are (1) Wiener, the founder of cybernetics, believes that information is neither matter nor energy, "information is information," "Information is the name of the content that people exchange with the external world in the process of adapting to the external world and making this adaptation react to the external world". (2) Shannon, the founder of information theory, also believes that information is a third thing distinct from matter and energy, and is an indeterminate description of the state of motion or the way of existence of things. However, in the process from spontaneous to conscious information, people found that information can be used to derive knowledge and data, and can be used to eliminate uncertainty. Information has become a "reflected material property". According to Professor Liu Xiaoying of Communication University of China, "Information is the reflection of the state and characteristics of all things."[143]

The characteristics of information are very similar to those of elementary particles in physics. The theory in physics holds that the smallest unit of matter, the elementary particle, becomes material once it is observed, and if it is not observed it is a wave, which is the wave-particle duality in theoretical physics. This characteristic, when introduced into the philosophy of science, allows us to think of information in such a way that if we think of it in two dimensions, one in the process of propagation and the other not in the process of propagation, we will find that information is observable when it is involved in the process of propagation, that is, when

---

[143] Liu Xiaoying,Dong Chao, 13 explanations about the development of contemporary media,"News Front, 2019, no. 17.

it is captured by another consciousness, is a "particle ", it is image-bearing, conceptualizable, material. When it is not involved in the propagation process, that is, when it is not captured by another consciousness, it is not observable, it is a "wave", it has no concrete symbolic image, it is not conceptualizable.

II. Information entropy

In the process of communication, the content in social media can be measured by the "information entropy". If we look at content from a scientific-philosophical point of view, content is a combination of information in many forms. In communication practice and research, it is obvious that there is no content in social media that is separate from communication, or it is not scientific to examine the content of social media separate from communication. According to the previous section, social media communication is a process of individual or collective consciousness interaction, and since information itself is generated by consciousness, the whole process of social media communication is an interactive process of consciousness. The consciousness pointed out here can be concretely expressed in various forms such as values, beliefs, thinking, focus of attention and perspective of observation. In the examination of social media, it is easy to find that "information entropy" can become a cross-cutting focus in the process of information dissemination, both from macro and micro aspects.The formation and development of the concept of "entropy" has gone through three stages: First, it was first constructed by the German physicist Clausius in 1865 as a state function to represent the second law of thermodynamics. Second, Boltzmann established a link between entropy and the number of possible microstates of a system, and gave a statistical explanation of the meaning of entropy; Schenon introduced the concept of entropy into information theory, taking entropy as a measure of uncertainty or information of random events, thus broadening the concept of entropy. Third, the concept of entropy went beyond its initial rigorous scientific application and was understood as a historical tendency reflecting the evolution of human thinking, called "generalized entropy". Over the past hundred years, the concept of entropy has deepened in generalization and rapidly penetrated into the natural and social sciences to solve problems in celestial evolution, biological evolution, and social development, becoming an important intersection of many disciplines.[144]"Entropy" is a continuous and discrete relationship, where discrete is a prerequisite for continuous and continuous is a result of discrete.

In 1948, Claude Shannon introduced the concept of "entropy" in thermodynamics into information theory and proposed the concept of "information entropy", which was originally used to measure the degree of disorder of a system in thermodynamics, but when applied to information theory, it is understood as a measure of "uncertainty". From the perspective of information theory, the higher the "entropy", the higher the uncertainty, the larger the information transmission, and the lower the "entropy", the lower the uncertainty, the smaller the information transmission. Therefore, the communication of social media is a process of changing "information entropy".

III. Information from "uncertainty

Thinking about the content of social media communication is also indeterminate when transferred to the philosophical perspective of quantum mechanics. Information, the smallest unit of communication, can be seen as a portion and a portion of energy in a discontinuous state. Discontinuity means that it is not traceable, cannot take continuous values, cannot be observed in physical quantities, and has to be expressed mathematically. The implications here are threefold: first, if one considers the human being as a collection of consciousness plus the senses, then from the point of view of information communication, the medium is an extension of the human senses, in the words of McLuhan, "the medium is an extension of the human being", or in the words of James Gleick, author of "A Brief History of Information " the human body itself is an information processor"; second, the ideal state of information dissemination between people, or communication between consciousness and consciousness, is barrier-free, direct, and without information loss. ;

---

[144] Cheng, Z. R. and Zhang Zhen, Implications of the Concept of Entropy for Economics, Journal of Zhengzhou University (Philosophy and Social Science Edition), 1992 (1)

third, language, words, images, expressions, actions, etc. can be used as a medium, i.e., the content to be expressed by consciousness The medium for symbolization, information can express consciousness, but not the whole picture of consciousness. Then, a complete communication process can be described as the following: a consciousness is created in the human mind that needs to be communicated -- the content of the consciousness is concretized, symbolized and formed into a message -- the message is attached to various carriers by language, words, images, expressions, actions, etc. -- transmitted to the receiving party.For example, if A sends a message on WeChat to say "hello" to B, then A must first create the consciousness of "hello" in his mind, and then choose the language symbol of "hello", which is transmitted to B through WeChat. Modern brain science believes that people have or create countless consciousnesses in their brains all the time, and when they need to spread, they will symbolize their consciousnesses and form messages, and then put the messages on some kind of carrier to spread. Based on the above process, we can conclude that in the communication activities of human society, information is the symbolization of consciousness, information is an expression of consciousness, and the symbol that can express consciousness is the first tool for communication and dissemination between people.[145]

In short, from the perspective of philosophy of science, the important aspects of our understanding of information should be the uncertainty of the content itself, the uncertainty of the communication process and the "information entropy" with a unified understanding.

---

[145] Dong Chao, Rules of information communication from the perspective of spatio-temporal dimension, Modern Communication (Journal of Communication University of China), February 2018

COMMUNICATION CHANNEL LEVEL: SPATIAL AND TEMPORAL DIMENSION

As mentioned earlier, social media is a media channel established based on human social interactions. In a broad sense, everything built on social relationships can be called social media, such as letters, oral messages, etc. However, this paper examines social media mainly in a narrow sense based on Internet technology, and the explanation here is limited to the level of network channels since the emergence of the Internet.

I. Social media communication channels are the "gas pedal" of information

Social media is the carrier of information communication in social networks, and is a network communication platform that users spontaneously participate in making and sharing. Since the birth of the Internet, social media has existed like a shadow, and the form of media on the Internet is constantly changing, and the timely information interaction platform is constantly changing from OICQ established in 1992, MSN established in 1995, WeChat established in 2011, etc. From voice chat platforms to video chat platforms, from shopping platforms such as Jingdong, Taobao and Tmall, to sharing communities such as blogs, microblogs and Zhihu, it is easy to see that the social media channels have moved from interpersonal information interaction to information integration and processing, from the initial pure communication platform to an information integration and selling platform that relies on social relationships and even expands social relationships, which is characterized by The number of information exchanged has increased from less to more, and the way of information expression has changed from text to image to a multimedia structure combining text, image, sound and other forms, and more importantly, the expansion of social networks and the speed of communication has been accelerated. A simple example is that the salt grabbing fiasco that started in Japan's nuclear leak on March 14, 2011, only reached its peak within 3 days and the rumors declined within 5 days, while the fiasco of grabbing Shuanghuanglian oral medicine in the

Wuhan COVID-19 in 2020 reached its peak late at night on the day of the report on January 31 and subsided the next morning. Monitoring shows that the public opinion cycle of sudden hotspot events in China was generally about two weeks before 2010, about a week around 2015, and only a day or two at present. It can be said that the law of change that has occurred in the communication channels of social media is that the speed of information communication has accelerated, not only in terms of the amount of information carried per unit of time, but also in the form of the way information is presented. Of course, this is also related to the increase of network speed and the continuous improvement of bandwidth.

II. Social media communication channels are "dimensional converters"

As mentioned earlier, we see information as a symbolization of consciousness, and people exist in four-dimensional space-time. Social media communication channels, such as WeChat, Weibo, and even Tmall and Taobao, are all tools to downscale information from higher dimensions . Dimension has different ways of understanding in different fields, for example, dimension in mathematics refers to the vector of measurement, space-time dimension in physics refers to space plus time, dimension in philosophy and social science refers to the perspective of thinking, and the space-time dimension referred to in this paper refers to the three dimensions of space plus a time dimension. Human existence is composed of a spatial dimension consisting of length, width and height, plus a forward time line, while the often mentioned four dimensions refer to three spatial dimensions plus a time dimension, so the spatio-temporal state of human existence is a dimension consisting of three-dimensional space and flowing time. The dimension of communication focuses on two aspects, on the one hand, the dimension of the existence of the message itself and the dimension of the message in the process of communication, and on the other hand, the dimensional properties of the medium. As argued before, information itself has the possibility to exist out of the timeline because it is the symbolization of consciousness. Information can be observed and used mainly because it is in the state of being downscaled in the process of communication, that is to say, the higher dimensional information is downscaled through the medium to become the information we can spread and the role played by the medium in it is the role of downscaling. Therefore, in the study of social media communication, the author believes that the channels of social media communication can be regarded as the tools to reduce the dimensionality of information. In the process of social media communication, information downscaling is an inevitable phenomenon. The communication of human society is done by people, regardless of the middle using big data, machine computing and other methods, the final completed communication is to achieve human and human information interaction, human and human information interaction is inevitably inseparable from the limitations of the spatio-temporal dimension, that is, the limitations of the linear flow of time. No matter what dimension the information exists in, as long as there is a need for communication, it is inevitable to carry out three-dimensional communication, which is inevitable to carry out communication practice in accordance with the way humans can communicate and accept. In the past communication studies, researchers have been neglecting this one issue, and temporal linearity, as the most important temporal cornerstone of communication, has not been sufficiently recognized. In the communication practice of social media, we can often observe the phenomenon that the huge amount of information, especially in the era of information overload now, is not only exploding, but simply blowing up, and all media are finding the information that meets their needs from the huge amount of information, and reconstructing it into a flow of information that can be spread linearly, and presenting it to the communicated, so that it can be read without time barriers. It can be said that the most important natural barrier that limits the communication of information is time, and the fixed limited time of human life and the linearity of information flow are the important cornerstones of social media communication.

III. The awareness of the channel brought about by the thinking

Looking at social media communication channels from the perspective of the spatio-temporal dimension leads to two findings: information acceleration and inevitability annihilating contingency.

The first is information acceleration. As the important feature of social media communication channel is to downscale information to become the information that can be spread by human society, then increasing the amount of information that can be spread per unit time and shortening the time of downscaling become the driving force of the change in media technology. First, the number of information that can be disseminated per unit of time, is completed by the speed of information media, greater bandwidth faster speed of dissemination becomes a powerful demand for the media to move forward, from 2G to 5G to bring the content of the change can be seen more clearly. Secondly, the time of information downscaling is being shortened, from information production to big data, from robot writing to artificial intelligence, this trend can also be seen clearly, the advance of social media is along the road of gradually shortening the time of information downscaling.

The second is the annihilation of chance by necessity in information communication. As the name implies, chance is unpredictable and necessity is predictable. Serendipity is an induction based on the unknown of human time advancement. The so-called serendipity is unknown and may be reached, and the so-called inevitability is known and necessarily reached. The information communication activities of human society were governed by chance before the emergence of the Internet. After the Internet, the inevitability of information communication was revealed, especially after the emergence of mobile Internet, many areas of chance were replaced by inevitability. For example, before the emergence of DDT, it was an accidental event, but it was changed by the new form of information communication, and standing on the roadside waiting for a car became inevitable after being positioned by accurate information and not only in the field of taking a taxi, we found that many accidental areas of life are being reshaped by inevitable information, so when we examine these phenomena, we can clearly see that it is information communication that turns accidentality into inevitability, and the important explanation behind it is the change of dimensionality. The disappearance of time linearity brings time solidification and non-fluidity, and time solidification makes the chance in life disappear.

"Self-Media and the Multiverse" at the level of communication audience

Audience is a changing concept, and the characteristics of audience are different in different media era, as far as audience research is concerned, our understanding of audience is also in constant change. However, most of the explanations in the past were made at the level of psychology and sociology, etc. If we look at the concept of audience from the perspective of philosophy of science, there may be an answer to another dimension of explanation. We can say that the audience is actually an individual whose consciousness is transmitted, and "the human body itself is an information processor". In the past, due to the limitation of media technology, it embodied the characteristics of monolithic, and the audience that was monolithic in the past is gradually completing the process of individualized splitting through the change of media technology. Each audience is an information world, and it is because of the revolution of mobile Internet technology that it is possible for each conscious body to build its own information world.

I. The self-information world composed of consciousness

As mentioned earlier, the concept of consciousness itself is highly controversial. In fact, the consensus that can be reached by setting aside the controversy is that consciousness is a combination of thoughts, feelings, sensations, and emotions. Every person's behavior is governed by consciousness, and every person is a conscious body. What we can observe in social media communication is that everyone is interpreting life and the world around them from their own perspective. Each person is wrapped in one or another social media based on Internet technology, and these media are "extensions of the person". In this new extension, unlike in McLuhan's time, the medium becomes a platform for the interactive mediation of information that is forming the world of self-media. Although some scholars believe that the creators of these messages are intentionally constructing "information cocoons," we conclude that if we look at the communicators or receivers separately, from the perspective of the initiative of the information processors, we can also say that each communicator is constructing its own information world around its own consciousness through the new media. What we habitually call media is actually an "engineering team" that builds its own information world, acquiring information, processing information, and releasing information, each person as a separate consciousness is building its own information world.

McLuhan's theory that "the medium is an extension of the person" needs to be further extended in the state of social media to say that "the medium is an extension of the person's consciousness". The eyes, ears, nose, tongue, body, and even mental activities are all innate mediums, and most of the tools developed by people are extensions of these sense organs. When modern information technology is developed today, the media technology revolution is a revolution of information processing technology one at a time. Internet, 5G, social media, APP, all these tools, are completing the work of building a unique information world around personal consciousness.

II. Unified propagation space-time and multiple propagation space-time

Before the emergence of social media, the communication of information in human society tended to be uniform and point-to-point, undertaken by professional media organizations, where individual awareness was fully manifested, which was not very easy to achieve technically. But all this has changed since the emergence of social media. With the leap in media technology, all kinds of new media and self-media are swarming, and the information wave is surging, as Professor Hu Yong exclaimed in his book "The Sound of the Crowd", "This is no longer an era when a thousand words converge into a single sentence". According to statistics, as of 2019, the number of annual active users on Face book is 2.3 billion, on QQ is 800 million, on WeChat is 1 billion, and on Youtube is 1.9 billion. All of these active individuals are a self-media, not only the endpoint of information communication and reception, but also the people who build their own information space-time world. One of the characteristics demonstrated by these phenomena is that unity has been deconstructed to a certain extent. A unified information world has been deconstructed into billions of independent information world units, and structuralism is the philosophy of the Internet, where the world is free and open. But we also found in the past communication practice, these unique information world units are sometimes gathered and sometimes scattered, sometimes share a theme, and sometimes in the independent weaving of their own "information cocoon".Unity and multiplicity coexist in the current media environment, which can be described by the "cloud concept" of the Internet, where a single water molecule can form a "cloud" only under certain conditions, and then return to the state of a water molecule after completing the task of rain. In fact, the concept of "multiverse" in string theory of quantum mechanics may better explain this self-media phenomenon. The multiverse is an explanation of the late development of quantum mechanics, which was proposed in 1955 and was silent for more than ten years, and then started to attract much attention after it was propagated by de Witt in 1967.[146]The string theory believes that the most basic unit in the universe is actually a small section of "energy strings", from large to interstellar galaxies, from small to gardenia quarks, all are such "energy strings". The world is composed of multidimensional space, and is also composed of multiple parallel universes, and the Earth is actually not alone. This way of explanation is recognized by many scientists, but there are also many questions, mainly because it is difficult to test with the current experimental conditions, but it does not prevent us from reflecting on social disciplines based on this kind of physics thinking.For example, we can understand that the world of information communication is a world composed of countless people or countless consciousnesses, who are building their own information world through communication and exchanging information with the world at the same time. At the theoretical level, there are as many information worlds as there are people, and as many information worlds as there are people involved in communication. The media technology or social media channels are just constantly and perfectly constructing the information world constituted by each consciousness.

In this way, the way we look at information communication has

---

[146] T. P. He and X. F. Qiao, Everett: the creator of the many-worlds interpretation of quantum mechanics, Journal of Shanxi University (Philosophy and Social Sciences Edition), January 2014

changed. According to the explanatory perspective of this paper, the information technology revolution brings not only a deconstructive change to information communication, but also a reductive one. Human information communication itself, which is the communication of self-information world with consciousness as the core, had to be unified due to the limitation of communication technology, but due to the revolution of communication technology, human information communication tends to be reverted back to the original world of personal information based on individual consciousness. At present, we are in the process of this reduction, seeing the intermingling of the real world and the virtual world, the interweaving of unified information and self-media information communication, but we can also clearly observe a trend of separation, that is, the development direction of human information communication activities will tend to be more in the direction of the self-information world, and the real world and the virtual world will show clear boundaries more and more.

III. The principle of attention conservation under time linearity

If we look at the issue of audience at the micro level from the perspective of philosophy of science, there exists a hypothetical premise that needs to be taken seriously, that is, whether it is in accordance with some principle of conservation, and in what respect the micro audience can manifest absolute conservation, which is the reflection of classical physics leading to philosophical social science. Information communication is like a force to the audience, in what direction is this force conserved? Or rather, there is no conservation for the microscopic, individual audience, but since we explain social media communication from a scientific-philosophical perspective, we must find a basis of conservation as a starting point, otherwise we cannot build an explanatory system. By constancy, the absolute "equality" of audiences in the dimension of examination. According to the above discussion of the spatio-temporal dimension, it is clear that the individual audience is consistent in time, attention is constant, because the human existence of space-time is three-dimensional, time is fluid, so the individual person is consistent only in time. A fixed examination cycle, each person's time is not increased or decreased, each person's day is 24 hours, each hour is 60 minutes, although time is a regulated concept, a consensus that may not really exist, but does not prevent us from using this consensus when interpreting at the philosophical-sociological level.Ignoring the personal will of individuals to disseminate and receive information for the time being, it will be found that the common feature of all people is to have a fixed time. We can understand that under the condition of time linearity, for information communication, time is the uniform standard of attention, and the attention of each audience is consistent and conservative within the fixed examination cycle. So the media is competing for and using the audience's time, making the audience's time a kind of capital and completing commercialization. This argument has long been studied by communication scholars, sociologists, and especially scholars of the political economy school, such as Herbert Schiller and his father, both of whom proposed the idea of digital capitalism. It can be said that human attention is an important capital for the commercial use of media, and attention is a contested resource. Under the condition of the existence of massive information, which media's information to read and which media's viewpoint to accept becomes the focus of attention contention, so the competition for audience's attention resources in the process of social media communication has become the most important battlefield. According to Sunstein, in choosing information sources, social media has achieved filtering for us, choosing media publishers that we are closer to, and this tendency is further deepened in the content of information that media choose in order to cater to the preferences and needs of the audience, which means that we only listen to what we choose and what pleases us.[147]In fact, from the yellow journalism of the late 19th and early 20th centuries to the current post-truth and emotional communication, the competition is for the attention of the audience, whose attention, because it is limited, is precious.

---

[147] Keith R. Sunstein, Information Utopia, Beijing,Law Press, 2008, p. 8

EMOTIONS, SCENARIO TRANSMISSION: UNCERTAINTY AND PROBABILITY

One of the important features of social media communication in today's era is "presence", which can also be called "virtual presence" as the digitalization process accelerates, where reason and emotion together form the "information dissemination field " where emotions and scenes coexist. The concept of "presence" here has two levels of meaning: "spatial presence" and "temporal presence". The spatial presence refers to the virtual communication space constructed by the media, and the "presence" is carried by the topic or the already constructed communication environment, such as the "yellow vest movement in France", "death vans in the UK", and "election in the US""U.S. Elections", etc. ".Chinese audiences are more active in social media, immersing themselves in the space constructed by the media even though they are thousands of miles away. Temporal presence means that, at a more macro level, social media is a means of enriching information in interaction, which dissolves the process of short-term communication in the traditional media period, and the information construction involved in social media is all of a longer duration, or it can be said to ignore temporality, while traditional media information communication is based on events and time to move forward, while information communication in the social media period is based on subject and interest.From the perspective of both time and space, the audience is immersed in the media field of space and time, and is present, involved and happy throughout the whole process.

I. Social media communication is necessarily emotional, emotions are also real

Emotion is a response derived from objective stimuli, and according to the brain neuroscientist Antonioni Damasio in his book Descartes' Error, emotion can be understood as a rational shortcut in the evolution of human beings.[148]Two aspects of this view are worth noting: one is that emotion is an objective manifestation, and the other is that behavior and emotion do not constitute an absolutely necessary relationship; there is emotion without necessarily having behavior, and there is behavior without necessarily having emotion. In the communication practices of social media, we can often observe the involvement of emotions, which are banished in the system of journalism. Journalism requires that what is stated be objectively true and that the views expressed be based on objective truth. However, when examining journalism in the traditional media, one finds that class and position attributes are inescapable in both East and West, that is, collective consciousness and collective emotions are fully involved in journalism. In fact, in traditional media, emotions should have existed and been recognized as objective elements. In the practice of social media, emotions have been an important element to examine and have been in the field of communication studies for a long time. Emotions have always been considered as a negative factor, and in the "post-truth" era, the lack of truth has been attributed to emotions, which has been explained as "too much emotion and not enough truth". However, it must be clear that there is an objective need to address emotions as an independent and important element of communication. Emotions themselves are not good or bad, but how to recognize them, use them, guide them and even dance with them is the focus of research.

The outbreak of the COVID-19 from December 2019 to early 2020. From the data of the RCU Newsroom team studying the phenomenon of the spread of this epidemic, it is clear that we can reflect the emotional drive from the official to the private sector.

---

[148] Antonioni Damasio, Descartes' Error, Beijing Union Publishing Company, 1st edition, February 2018, based on a summary of the interpretation of the whole book studying consciousness, sensation, and perception.

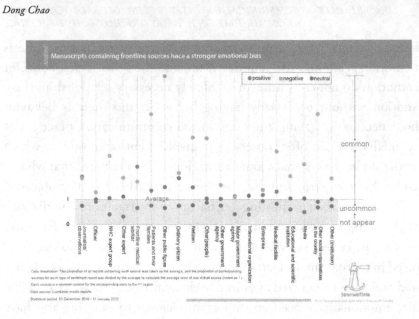

Chart 3.1

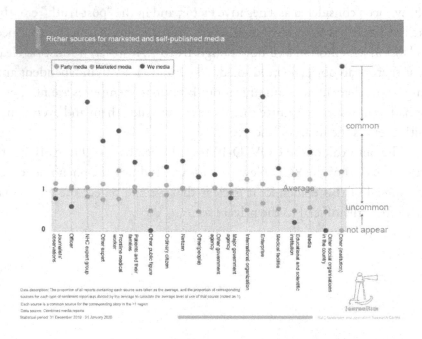

Chart 3.2

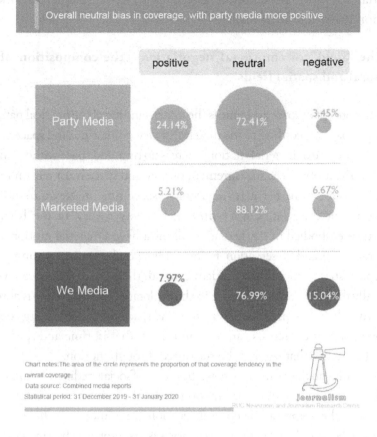

Chart 3.3

Through the above three data charts, it is obvious to conclude that emotions are shaping the content and direction of communication. It even forms a fracture between individual emotions and official information. Social media is a media collection with a strong tendency of individualization, and individual emotions are more likely to be expressed and can form an exponential influence on communication. In our analysis of emotions, we pointed out that the theory of "emotional contagion" in psychology is particularly applicable in social media. As a contagious and reproducible element, emotions spread rapidly in social media. In fact, emotions are a kind of social network reality, and this reality also includes objective reality, because emotions are derived from the "picking" of the truth by the self. In social media, for the audience, the truth is only the material that proves the emotion he receives, so we say that in social media, emotion is also a kind of reality.

II. The "field" of emotional negotiation - the composition of the temporal and spatial fields

The concept of space and time is the understanding of the physical nature of time and space. According to the materialist viewpoint, time and space are the form of existence of material motion, there is no time and space without matter and material motion, the measurement of time and space must rely on matter as the measure. Whether it is the absolute space-time in Newton's classical mechanics, or the relative space-time in relativity theory, or the Riemann space-time embodied in mathematics, all must have a material motion as the basic reference and observation point. Although the understanding of the concept of space-time, in the academic world, there are still disparate views, especially the philosophy of science in the exploration of space-time is absolute or relative, the relationship between time and space there is still a large debate, but one point of consensus can be determined, that is, time and space are a kind of existence that needs to be measured through motion.

According to the materialist view, the metric of social media communication should be the movement of information itself. The movement of information constitutes the information communication time and space fields.[149] Field theory can be introduced here. Field theory was first proposed by physicists such as Kauffka in the 19th century, but was introduced into the field of sociology by Bourdieu and others. The "field" of social media communication in this paper contains the following elements: information in motion, structured information interaction, horizontal and vertical combination of time[150], and the flow of virtual space. Information communication in social media is the interactive flow of information in the field of time and space, and forms a unique structure. In our perceivable world, the spatio-temporal scope of information flow is constant in the temporal perspective and flows along the timeline. This

---

[149] Some scholars have also expressed the information time field and information space field as "media time" and "media space".

[150] The concept of "horizontal and vertical combination" is borrowed from Saussure's concept of "equilibrium combination" and "vertical combination" in the four groups of dichotomies.

flow contains two dimensions, a linear flow within an examination cycle and the ability of its information communication themes to flow in ephemeral time. In space, this range of perception is a combination of the real and the virtual, which in the future may move towards a deeper integration or even a self-contained separation due to the technological revolution. From a scientific-philosophical point of view, the only metric that can judge the spatio-temporal field is the information in the interaction. The information in motion and readable is the only metric of the spatio-temporal field.

In social media, the interaction of information is emotionally involved, and the technological change of social media has brought about the construction of self-information worlds, so the interaction of information in social media is the construction of "self-information worlds" in time and space. This kind of communication is characterized by strong subjectivity and emotionality. If we bring the "self-information world" with emotion into the longitudinal time field, we will find that when we examine each person's communication, there is an emotional coherence, and the performance of "narrative makes time fragrant"[151]is obvious from the jump of personal emotion to following others' views. Organized social media, such as official media platforms, tend to be more consistent, with smooth and clear emotions, and when the emotions are brought into ephemeral communication, they are regular and universal, no matter how long it takes, although more social media platforms show jumps and instability. "The end of narrative carries with it a temporal dimension of consequence. It puts an end to linear time. Events are no longer continuous as a history." [152]Bringing emotions into the spatial field reveals that communication is more active in virtual space and cold in real communication. It can be said "Thinking interferes with the probability of possible events."[153]In the process of social media communication, emotions are negotiated in the temporal and spatial fields of the "self-information world" of an individual or an organization.

---

[151] Han Bingzhe, Bao Xiangfei et al, The Taste of Time, Chongqing University Press, December 2017, p. 42

[152] Han Bingzhe, Bao Xiangfei et al, The Taste of Time, Chongqing University Press, December 2017, p. 41

[153] David L. Watson, "Entropy and Organization," Science 72 (1930):222. p280, cited in, [U.S.] James Gleick, A Brief History of Information, People's Post and Telecommunications Press, 1st edition (16th printing, August 2018),December 2013,p.265

THE LEVEL OF PROPAGATION RELATIONS: QUANTUM CORRELATIONS BETWEEN THE HYPERDISTANCE AND THE TRANSCENDENTAL

The network society is a society where the social relations of communication are changing dramatically, and the priority of relationship is an important law in social media communication. Then how should we understand the transmission relationship on social media, the sentific-philosophical point of view can also help us.

I. The relationship and characteristics of social media communication

The relationship of social media communication is essentially a relationship between people and people, who are also divided into individuals and groups, and groups refer to media organizations, such as large media, self-media operation teams, etc. For better description, the relationship can be seen as a combination of three relationships, namely, the relationship between individuals and individuals, the relationship between individuals and groups, and the relationship between groups and groups. By putting these three groups of relationships into a huge communication network, a new structure of information communication relying on social networks is formed.

In social media, this communication relationship is characterized by at least three features. The first feature is that the power of communication is balanced, and the audience is empowered in terms of information choice. In the traditional media era, the transmission-receiving relationship was still "strong transmission and weak reception", but after entering the social media era, this relationship has changed .The power of communication has been repeatedly weakened, and the choice of the receiver has been repeatedly strengthened, and people choose information that we tend to trust more. This phenomenon also existed in the traditional media era, but after entering the social media era, people have the right to choose in the face of the constant explosion of information, choosing only the information they can accept and blocking all other information on their own. development tends to be toward the equalization of transmission and reception. The second characteristic is that superimposed social relationships promote the richness of information communication. Social media is a form of media that relies on social relations, and social relations in human society are never flat. In terms of social relations, some scholars believe that western social relations are like a pair of tied chopsticks, each independent and tied by rules, while eastern social relations are like what Fei Xiaotong calls ripples. Casting family-based stones on a calm lake creates ripples of relationships, and ripples and ripples influence each other, so social interaction relationships are never simple single lines from A to B and B to C. They are multiple and superimposed. The communication of social media is also three-dimensional, and it is information communication based on complex relationships, and such complex relationships directly determine the influence and richness of information. The third characteristic is the tendency of social media information communication to be non-logical. Logicalization refers to deterministic thinking that can be deduced, while illogicalization means that it cannot be explained by conventional logic and needs to borrow other ways of description. There has always been an argument against anti-Rogosianism in the study of philosophy, and a critique of logicalism prevails in the philosophical community to this day. When we look at social media communication phenomena, such as the Trump campaign in the United States, the conflict between the United States and Iran, the United Kingdom's exit from the European Union, and so on, we will find that it is often the emergence of a theme that causes the buzz, in which many prominent events, details or comments are able to resonate with people, achieving a relatively wide communication effect. This "resonance" is the theme element of social media communication, that is to say, a social media event, when entering the personal interpretation system, once the interpretation and the way to receive the same, it will produce the resonance across the distance ignoring the identity of the transmission and the recipient. For example, when Donald Trump was elected president of the United States, according to the research data in the United States, a large part of the people who spread and tweeted their opinions on Facebook and Twitter were not native American users, and even many rumors were organized in Eastern European countries. So beyond the conventional spatial distance and break the conventional logical way, is the more common characteristics of social media communication.

II. Trans-distance, trans-experience, association: an explanation of the philosophy of science of communication relations

Through the above research observation, it can be found that if from the perspective of the philosophy of science, the transmission-reception relationship of social media communication can be seen as having three characteristics: trans-distance, trans-experience and entanglement. First of all, the trans-distance refers to the spatial trans-distance nature of social media communication, which is at the level of physical meaning, referring to the ability of the trans-distance action of real space-time. This relationship is a typical result of the change of the physical carrier of information communication, and the technological development of human information communication has been an effort to break the time and space barriers, from paper media to radio, from electronic signals to the Internet, from 1G to 5G,the main task of information communication is to break the spatial and temporal barriers to human communication through media technology. Second, the trans-experience) character. The basic meaning of "trans-experience)" is to exceed experience without leaving it, and also to make the realization of experience possible.[154]According to Professor Wu Guolin, the basic connotation of trans-experience includes being beyond the old experience to form a new experience, and being able to make the experience possible.[155]It can be considered that trans-experience is a kind of dimensional enhancement of the knowledge of things. Professor Guolin Wu also believes that trans-experience is in line with materialism and dialectics. In the study of social media, we can understand that phenomena and theories (obtained through existing experiences) are a pair of binary systems with rapid turnover, borrowing the way of thinking from

---

[154] Guolin Wu, Transcendence and Quantum Interpretation, Chinese Social Sciences, February 2019
[155] Guolin Wu, Transcendence and Quantum Interpretation, Chinese Social Sciences, February 2019

materialistic dialectics is that the accumulation of experience and theories are mutually influencing relationships, and theories are obtained through experience and also beyond empirical cognition, but when new experiences have not yet been formed, theories at this time have the characteristic of "trans-experience". Phenomena and cognition are a dynamic binary structure that rapidly contributes to the formation of new understanding. Such a characteristic exists in the transmission-reception relationship of social media communication, in which both the transmission and reception sides rely on experience to complete their understanding and enrich it by recognizing and selecting already experienced phenomena. However, since the rate of information transmission in social media is gradually accelerating, which includes the increase of content, the change of interaction rate, and the increase of information interaction, the time of facing information, selecting information, and forming awareness is also accelerating, so the characteristic of "trans-experience" is formed.Finally, the characteristics of "correlation" can be borrowed from the theory of "quantum correlation". In quantum mechanics, a pair of correlated quanta, no matter how distant they are, can produce a kinematic reaction regardless of the speed of light. The observation and determination of this phenomenon are derived from physics experiments and theoretical derivations, and will not be described more specifically here. The explanation of this phenomenon is also of philosophical interest. One explanation is the "string theory" in quantum mechanics and the "superstring theory" that was developed later, i.e., the observation of the spatio-temporal dimension beyond the scope of our experience to find an explanation. Although "string theory" is controversial, it does not prevent scholars of philosophy of science from thinking about it philosophically. If we observe the phenomenon of social media communication, we will find that there are many communication phenomena that are not in the linear logic of our existing communication theories, for example, we used to think that the flow of information and information is a continuous process, but based on this understanding, we will get different answers. In practice, it is always possible to see events that go beyond linear communication logic. For example, Trump's election and Yiwu Commodity City have nothing to do with each other, but there are reports that Yiwu Commodity City was the first place to know about Trump's election because there were far more Trump banners than

Hillary in Yiwu orders, which is an example of quantum correlation. The list of similar examples goes on and on. So, the relationship between two information communicators has the characteristic of not being related in real life space, but will always be related in the information world. This is also a reflection of the characteristics of relationships in social media.

QUESTION THEORY
EXPLANATION OF
INFORMATION SPACE
MEDIA COMMUNICATION

CHAPTER 4

A SYSTEM OF SCIENTIFIC-PHILOSOPHICA EXPLANATION OF SOCIAL MEDIA

In the previous chapter, we tried to explain some new features arising from the development of social media using relevant concepts from the philosophy of science. In this chapter, we will try to establish an overall explanatory framework, including an explanation of the most basic unit in social media --- information, an explanation of the effectiveness of social media communication, an explanation of the essential features and basic functions of social media, and an overview of the social media explanation system, and at the end of this chapter, we also try to establish a formula for the effectiveness of social media information communication.

QUANTUM THEORY'S EXPLANATION OF INFORMATION IN SOCIAL MEDIA COMMUNICATION

Information, the most basic unit of communication, should be said that the knowledge of information, we also continue to deepen, to know the information of the network era, is the basis of our understanding of social media.

I. Information as the symbolization of consciousness

There are two perspectives on the understanding of information ontology. One is the classical understanding based on reflection on classical mechanics: deterministic, linear, and continuous. The second is the non-classical interpretation based on reflection of quantum mechanics: probabilistic and discontinuous. The understanding of classical mechanics means that the change of information is with continuity, and the non-classical understanding of quantum mechanics, where the information is discontinuous and non-traceable, taking values and studying the understanding, should stand in the perspective of discontinuity. Scholars of philosophy of science have studied and found that the description and expression of knowledge of the world through quantum theory starts from the knowledge of the quantum itself, the most fundamental constituent unit of the world. From an etymological point of view, the word "quantum" comes from the Latin word "quantus", which means "how much" and is an expression of a definite quantity, which can be understood as a themeasure of independent energy. In quantum mechanics, it refers to a fundamental unit of energy or a small, indivisible amount of energy.[156] According to the summary of scholars of philosophy of science, it has undesirable continuous values, undesirable directly associated values, non-traceable, and can be migrated. The quantum-quantum correlation is non-classical, which is subversive to the traditional logical perception.

---

[156] Cheng, Sumei, A Philosophical Manifesto for Quantum Theory,Chinese Social Sciences,February 2019

Information, as the most basic unit in social media, also has multiple dimensions for its ontological understanding. From the information theory perspective information is bits, from the news communication perspective information is the smallest unit of communication, and this tiny unit is the basis of all information communication. Due to the emergence of social media, in addition to the symbolic character of information, the involvement of consciousness has become an important element before researchers. In physics, microscopic particles are also the most fundamental unit of the material world. Using the concept of microscopic particles in physics to compare the study of information in communication will yield enlightening and universal implications. If we compare the information in social media communication with the microscopic particles in physics, we will find that they have a large similarity. Firstly, at the level of action, both are the most basic units; secondly, at the level of composition, information is composed of consciousness and symbols, which eventually form the propagation force, while microscopic particles also have wave-particle duality. "Particles can be divided into two types: those that constitute matter are called fermions, and those that transmit forces are called bosons. The difference between the two is that fermions each occupy their own separate space, while bosons can be stacked together." [157] That is, it means that microscopic particles are composed of matter and the force of associated matter, where it is noteworthy that the force of associated matter is a force that can be measured precisely and can be stacked, and is called a boson. Information has similar structural characteristics, and the expressible symbols can be understood as fermions in particles, while the force of associated symbols is human consciousness, which also has the property of being superimposable without occupying space. Therefore, information and microscopic particles have the same characteristics and are comparable.

According to the interpretation of physics, human understanding of elementary particles has a long development process that can be divided into three stages. One is the conclusion reached during the ancient Greek period relying on discernment, and the second is the clarification of the

---

[157] Sean Carroll, The Particle at the End of the Universe: How the Hunt for the Higgs Boson Leads Us to the Edge of a New World, Hunan Science and Technology Press, January 2014, p. 23

material properties of elementary particles with the emergence of the Copernican revolution and Newtonian mechanics, and the emphasis on the nature of matter as continuously divisible. The third is the emergence of quantum mechanics, emphasizing that the elementary particles have wave-particle duality characteristics. And a comparison with people's understanding of information will reveal almost the same route taken. The new understanding of information started from the study of discernment, to the knowledge is power, and then to the new understanding of information. The physics community has clarified the formality of quantum mechanics and has shown that quantum theory also applies to the macroscopic world, so we can try to explain information itself in the context of the new propagation with the understanding of microscopic particles by quantum mechanics. In quantum theory, microscopic particles obey the principle of homogeneity and are indistinguishable, and two microscopic particles that once interacted with each other are still associated after separation, which is widely known as "quantum entanglement".[158]Matter is not infinitely divisible, nor is information infinitely divisible, nor does information obey the classical mechanics principle of infinite divisibility.

Accordingly, we can draw two conclusions, one is the extension of the understanding of "information as symbolic consciousness", the composition of information is symbol plus consciousness, forming a kind of communication force, and the magnitude of the force lies in the frequency of interaction with the information. Secondly, consciousness as a communicating symbolic force can be combined with the philosophical understanding of boson in quantum theory, which is superimposed, invisible, observable, measurable and immaterial. In communication practice we can also find numerous examples that can be explained in this perspective, that is, the more attention is paid to the same thing, it means that the consciousness is more involved, and then the more the thing has the power of communication.

---

[158] Guolin Wu, Transcendence and Quantum Interpretation, Chinese Social Sciences, February 2019

II. The social media communication structure of micro information

Since both symbols and consciousness are the basic power sources in social media communication, the structure of social media communication has two levels. One is that all social media communication is a symbol-plus-consciousness model, an interaction between symbols and consciousness. It can be understood that in social media communication, the theme formed by an event, there are transmitters and recipients together to form a lot of figurative symbols for communication, these symbols are associated by consciousness as a whole, which is a communication unit, or a communication meaningful information. The more the consciousness is involved, the greater the power of the message, and the less the consciousness is involved, the less the power of the message. In addition, the magnitude of the vibration of the message in the process of communication also reflects the power of communication. We can see in the social media communication of popular topics will find such a phenomenon, that is, on a topic in the timeline to see, the frequency of dissemination are high frequency, the speed of manufacturing information per unit of time is amazing. Unit time topics, themes, information manufacturing speed is the frequency, the greater the frequency, the stronger the power of communication. Secondly, the jumpiness of social media communication. According to the theory of quantum mechanics, the movement of microscopic particles is not traceable because it is discontinuous, and microscopic particles cannot be conceptualized, characterized, imagined, or observed.[159] That is, microscopic particles are not continuously expressible in the real world, which is inconsistent with our traditional understanding that they are all continuous. The relationship between information and information is discontinuous, and the relationship between symbols and symbols is also discontinuous; these are uncertainties in domination and have probabilistic characteristics. Therefore, the structure of information communication cannot be viewed in a continuous view, and each message can be seen as an independent block of energy with propagation power, and the association between messages is governed by probability to produce

---

[159] Cheng, Sumei, A Philosophical Manifesto for Quantum Theory,Chinese Social Sciences,February 2019

structure. This can also explain the phenomenon often seen in social media communication, where an event somehow becomes entangled with another communication event, while an event with the same properties does not become associated with this communication event. For example, Guo Meimei originally had nothing to do with the Red Cross, but because of its falsified relationship with the Red Cross, it has generated constant criticism of the Red Cross by society to this day. Then there is the case of DDT, an Internet company that in a few years defeated a cab company that is not an industry at all. The same social media communication event is always characterized by the "supramarginal choice" in economics, i.e., instead of looking for clues within the logical line of events, it starts from a completely different perspective. This "downscaling" comes from a non-classical logic of information dissemination, not a problem of linear logic, but the need to build another logic with more explanatory power based on classical logic, that is, probabilistic logic based on uncertainty.

III. Implications of quantum theory for understanding information

First, information is the basic unit of communication, information is consciousness and symbols through the composition. Information is what Wiener, Shannon and others believe that information itself does not have energy, information is information, and later proposed that information is bits, and in 1978 Wheeler even made his famous assertion that everything originates from bits. It is true that information itself does not have energy, but once it is involved in the process of communication, it is endowed with energy, and information space-time is the space-time of meaning.

Secondly, the power of information communication relies on the participation of more consciousness in the process of dissemination, and social media provides a wider space for the transmission of information between consciousnesses. The degree, frequency and amount of consciousness participation determine the spreading power of that information.

Finally, in the process of communication, information is independent and undesirable for continuous values. Discontinuity means untraceability, and a perfect communication model cannot be established empirically, but only on the basis of probability, and its communication effect is inevitably constrained by the probability.

EXPLANATION OF SOCIAL MEDIA COMMUNICATION EFFECTS BY PHILOSOPHY OF SCIENCE

Effect is the end of the last communication and the starting point of the next one, and effect is also the reason for the existence of communication. But from a scientific and philosophical perspective, the effect of social media communication also reflects a strong uncertainty and is often governed by a non-deterministic probability theory.

I. Uncertainty interpretation of social media communication

The original purpose of the study of quantum mechanics was to investigate by observation and experiment whether the smallest unit that makes up the world is a particle or a fluctuation. This question began in the 17th century when Newton laid down classical physics, and continued to be discussed in the 21st century with the research on quantum mechanics. As the double slit interference experiment, wave-particle duality was observed, and then Bell's inequality was broken, quantum entanglement, etc. were studied in depth, various experiments in theoretical physics proved that the smallest unit that makes up the world is fluctuation, and as of the current research in theoretical physics, it was concluded that in our empirical world, the human consciousness is involved in the nature of matter. The problems that originally belonged to physics entered the philosophical level, and what belonged to nature was directed to what belonged to consciousness. The human consciousness is banished and then make-up returns. Uncertainty is an understanding based on the extension of the fundamental properties of the quantum, which cannot take a definite value and is the point of view determined by quantum theory. This view can also be applied to our observation of social media.

First, in social media communication, the communication effect has uncertainty and is not desirable to have a fixed value. This thesis is more in line with the results of previous communication studies. In past studies, both powerful effect theory and limited effect theory have sought to find a theoretical explanation that can determine the effect of communication, and researchers have also designed various models for this purpose.[160]However, we cannot deny that no model can exhaustively describe and accurately predict the effects of communication. For this communication phenomenon, the group communication theory proposed by Professor Sui Yan of Communication University of China, which explores the characteristics of group communication based on the philosophy of chaos, has an enlightening view. Whether through the phenomenal observation of social media communication or through the theoretical observation of social media communication, it can be found that the uncertainty of the communication effect is instead the most certain, and there is no definite rule for the information communication effect. But even so, the communication effect is not indescribable and unintelligible. The uncertainty in quantum theory is an argument based on a definite mathematical formula, so the uncertainty can be explained and understood. On the contrary, it is not difficult to find that the main variables of uncertainty of the communication effect come from such contingent factors as the change of communication channels, the increase of complexity after the participation of more communication subjects, and other information interference, so if we want to take the definite value of uncertainty, we should use the method of Occam's razor to remove all the interference and find the objective measurement degree that necessarily exists in all social media information communication processes. Information arrival, so to speak, is a degree of measurement that meets objective criteria. In social media communication, only by objectively observing the degree of information arrival, it is possible to model the decisive influence between communication effects and objective criteria. For example, in the simple communication model of A and B, A sends a message to B. According to our criteria, only the degree of arrival is tested, and B is counted as having arrived whether or not it generates conscious thought or thought response after receiving the message, and A sends a hundred messages to B, and B is counted as having arrived whether or not it generates thought response after receiving the message. The Palo Alto school famously asserted that communication cannot determine how you think, but it can determine what you think. This has two connotations: the amount of information communicated, and the subject matter of the

---

[160] For details, you can refer to [English] Dennis McGuire's book "Theory of Mass Communication Model" Shanghai Translation Publishing House 1990.

information communicated. As mentioned above, the "conservation of attention" of the audience is a constant. 24 hours a day is the limit of the reading time for any audience to receive information. Although the current research cannot give a precise conclusion on how much information can contribute to the acceptance of B at the conscious level, it is possible to describe such a measure of information through this explanation.

Second, the uncertainty of information meaning generation in the communication process. We generally understand uncertainty mainly based on complexity, and uncertainty because of complexity. However, based on quantum theory, this uncertainty is intrinsic and has nothing to do with complexity and simplicity, not the uncertainty of too many variables that cannot be measured and predicted their structure, but an innate uncertainty. This uncertainty in quantum theory is derived from the smallest unit itself. In social media communication, this uncertainty arises from the message itself. The symbol is certain because the symbol is an agreed consensus, then the only uncertainty arises from the consciousness in information communication. In particular, the participants involved in information dissemination in social media are both individuals and organizations, and they have different positions, interests and other aspects. These subtle differences all produce different states of consciousness, and the information condensed into these states of consciousness are all involved in the process of information dissemination. As Carl Eckert said, "Thinking creates entropy", so a new power of communication on a certain theme or topic is formed. The complexity of the communication structure in this process, together with the uncertainty of the meaning of information itself, constitutes the uncertainty of information meaning generation in the communication process.

II. The probability explanation of social media communication effect

Many communication scholars have tried to describe a decisive roadmap for the study of information communication from different perspectives, but invariably found the odd phenomenon that there are always successes and failures, always accuracies and surprises, and that probability dominates the entire communication process. According to Wittgenstein, "Probability is a generalization. It involves a general description of a propositional form. It is only in the absence of certainty that we need probability. That is, when: we do not know a fact completely, but we do know something about its form."[161] In the same way that Einstein's theory of relativity in physics must rely on non-Euclidean geometry, the new propagation of research methods and thinking perspectives requires a new philosophical interpretation, which is the probabilistic way of thinking about uncertainty and indeterminacy. The philosophical description of uncertainty is that "it is impossible for the uncertainty principle to confirm some statement of ...... about intermediate phenomena"[162] and "we cannot find a normal system for all intermediate phenomena, but for each intermediate phenomenon a normal system can be found." [163] The explanation of uncertainty can be done using a probabilistic approach, or what Reichenbach calls the theory of three values. In his book The Philosophical Foundations of Quantum Mechanics, the German scholar Reichenbach states that "whereas the Ball-Heisenberg interpretation uses a restricted meaning approach, we have conceived a second form of finite interpretation, which uses three-valued logic. Ordinary logic is written in terms of two truth values, namely true and false. To these two, for the purposes of quantum mechanics, we added a third truth value called indeterminacy." [164] Uncertainty is seen as a true value introduced into the field of philosophy and can also be used as a basis for thinking into social media communication thinking.

The social media communication effect itself is a probability problem with uncertainty. The probability referred to here is currently still a non-computable understanding that needs mathematical support from later studies. "What probability itself actually means ...... The objectivist school insists that the probability of a fact occurring is the nature of the event itself ...... The subjectivist view, on the other hand, holds that probability is a belief about how an event might will happen how it

---

[161] Wittgenstein, A Treatise on the Philosophy of Logic, The Commercial Press, 2014, p. 66

[162] H. Reichenbach, Philosophical Foundations of Quantum Mechanics, The Commercial Press, 2015 (reprinted 2018), p. 65

[163] H. Reichenbach, Philosophical Foundations of Quantum Mechanics, The Commercial Press, 2015 (reprinted 2018), p. 52

[164] H. Reichenbach, Philosophical Foundations of Quantum Mechanics, The Commercial Press, 2015 (reprinted 2018), pp.69-70

does."[165]of probability can be understood as follows: firstly, the probability of arrival of information communication, the probability of arrival of information is mainly dependent on the technology itself, the stability of social media communication hardware such as information transmission technology, information receiving hardware, information terminals such as APP reading method, notification method, etc. are all restrictions on the probability of arrival; secondly, the probability of information communication being read and understood completely. The probability of being read and understood is whether the information can be read and understood completely in a fixed time domain, which is required by the short-term effect of communication; finally, the probability of the information being re-disseminated, after the information recipient receives the information, the feedback of the information includes two actions of internalization and re-dissemination and accepting but no longer disseminating is to interrupt the dissemination in a fixed time domain, so Internalization and re-propagation is a probabilistic problem.

In addition to the complex influences of hardware, it is the consciousness itself that governs the probability of the propagation effect. Whether the consciousness of the message receiver responds to a message or not is the focus of determining the probability of message propagation.

III. The third logic of social media communication

Traditional information communication is based on time logic. The communicator spreads according to time, the receiver receives according to time, and the presentation of all communication contents is also carried out according to the logic of time. It can be said that before the emergence of online media, the logic of human information communication was event logic at the surface level and time logic at the deep level. However, this logic has been deconstructed by online media communication practices, and this deconstruction is especially prominent after the emergence of social media. Since social media are high-dimensional media that do not rely on linear communication space-time existence, there is also a third communication logic of social media communication, which is the logic of

---

[165] Tom Siegfried, Nash Equilibrium and Game Theory, Chemical Industry Press, July 2018, p. 141

association, a logic of information association in which the consciousness of the transmitter-recipient is the associated body.

First, the traditional logic of events, which appears to be a necessary causal logic, is in fact a probabilistic logic that is not fully understood. Reichenbach argues that "if causality is described as the limit of the relation of probability implication ...... the causal principle can only be retained as an empirical hypothesis." [166] This is a reflection on the philosophical level of science, where the traditional event logic is that all things in an event and the information disseminated are in uninterrupted continuity, and in fact this correlation is essentially a probability-based correlation. As such high probability events are summarized in daily life experience and form simple causal thinking, but the core foundation behind it is still a probabilistic foundation, so event logic itself is a logic of high probability events.

Second, temporal logic is the dimensional basis of event logic. Event logic is based on causal logic, and the basis of causal logic is temporal logic, and it can be said that cause and effect are based on the linear flow of time. Time flows and contingency exists because it is unknowable and irreversible, so event logic also has this characteristic. Event logic is a logic built on unknowable and irreversible full of unknown contingencies. Before the emergence of online media, information communication relied on the event logic based on the logic of time, and all information generated after the occurrence of events was based on the linear flow of time. From the interpretation of the event itself, to the narrative and dissemination of the event, to the linearity of the information distribution channel, it can be said that the whole process of information communication is a construction based on the linearity of time accepted by the audience.

Again, the logic of social media association. As evidenced earlier, information itself is a reality that can exist in high dimensions, and the function of media is to downscale the high-dimensional information into the four-dimensional space-time of our lives, so that the information can produce a linear flow with time. In the traditional media period this state could be observed as a temporal logic with cause-and-effect relationship. But with the emergence of social media, this correlation begins to manifest

---

[166] H. Reichenbach, *Philosophical Foundations of Quantum Mechanics*, The Commercial Press, 2015 (reprinted 2018), p. 9

itself in a non-temporal manner. Cloud technology stores information in the cloud in a wide range, and when observed from the perspective of the user of information communication, one finds that this stored information has a high-dimensional character and is used in a downscaled manner only when a person needs it. This information includes what is already present, what has been recorded, and what is being produced. Since information is disjointed independent units, the consciousness of the communicator is involved in the process of combining information, and this combination is essentially done by relying on consciousness. Consciousness associates information, and the combination of information becomes the content of communication. If we consider this combination of information as another unit of information, it will be combined by the consciousness into a new structure, and so on. Therefore, social media communication has a third logic other than the logic of time and the logic of events, that is, the logic of association.

Finally, it is important to emphasize that social media communication reflects the combination of three logics, both the production and communication based on temporal logic and the high probability association of event logic, and also reflects the characteristics of association logic, social media communication is not independent of the existence of temporal logic and event logic, but only adds a communication logic, social media practice is actually a state of coexistence of three logics.

PHILOSOPHY OF SCIENCE ON THE ONTOLOGY AND FUNCTION OF SOCIAL MEDIA

In the process of the study of information and communication effects, we have actually touched upon the question of the ontology and function of social media. What kind of presence is social media and what kind of role does this presence play in society is also something that we need to account for in our system of explanation.

I. Social media is a high-dimensional media

From the perspective of human information communication history, the media has undergone a very clear development process, that is, constantly breaking through the spatial and temporal limitations of communication. Media is dimensional, and every communication era has a fixed communication dimension as a scope standard. According to the spatio-temporal dimension, we can divide the human communication history into, one-dimensional media period, two-dimensional media period, three-dimensional media period, four-dimensional media period. The division of media dimension is based on the premise of what kind of space-time the information breaks.

One-dimensional media: the oral communication period, information interaction is language transmission, the information does not break time and space, is the export into the ear of the communication relationship.

Two-dimensional media: the period of communication based on physical carriers, the main representative is the paper media, oracle bones, stone tablets and all other information recorded on physical carriers, the period of communication is characterized by breaking the physical space as well as part of the time in the human acceptable category.

Three-dimensional media: electronic technology as the premise of the media, such as radio, television and other media, the properties of this media is that information can be through this category of media across time and space, but it has a reading limit, the limit is the system must be the premise of the timeline, that is, must be consistent with the "human" three-dimensional space-time existence of biological characteristics, that is, the flow of time.[167]

Four-dimensional media: The social media based on the Internet for information communication is the four-dimensional media. This media era is to make information cross time and space limitations, and can freely interconnect and reach the reading terminal. But because the information is four-dimensional (which is an assumption), people in the three-dimensional world need to downscale the four-dimensional information before they can read it, which means that the interconnected information without the characteristics of time flow must be integrated into the form of information with linear time flow characteristics through the carrier, which is what promotes a variety of media presentation in the current society.

Therefore, from the perspective of media ontology, media is a carrier that raises and lowers the dimensionality of information. Media downscaling refers to the process of presenting the information stored in four-dimensional space-time to people in three-dimensional space-time through media technology. For example, applications such as Weibo and Today's Headlines connect information scattered in the network and push it to the audience in a linear reading manner. The personalization and popularization of media technology has given individuals the ability to freely downscale information, such as making their own choices about the content, arrangement, and presentation of information, which makes human interaction more proactive.

Media ascension refers to the ability of the media to disseminate information from three dimensions to four dimensions, while having the ability to downscale information in four dimensions to three dimensions and at the same time to ascend. Information being downgraded to three dimensions still carries the characteristics of four dimensions (i.e. causality disappears due to time fixation), and in the case of online media, the main function of this information downgradation is to turn all chance into necessity. For the observer in three-dimensional space-time, because of the linear flow of time, the fundamental characteristic of the "future" that did not happen is chance. In four-dimensional space-time, time is as

---

[167] Cao Tianyuan, The History of Quantum Physics[M], Shenyang: Liaoning Education Press, 2011 edition

fixed as length, width, and height, and the uncertainty brought by time disappears, and all chance becomes necessity. When the information with this property is downscaled to three-dimensional space-time, it has an ascending influence on real life because it carries the characteristics of four-dimensional space-time, and the ascending characteristics of network media begin to appear. For example, applications or platforms such as GPS, DDT, Meituan takeaway, etc. are mastering the information ascension characteristics of network media and making full use of the inevitability of information, thus eliminating the chance in three-dimensional space-time to a certain extent. Simply put, the network media turns the chance in daily life into the inevitability in four-dimensional space.

To understand the property of "social media as four-dimensional media", we need to grasp the following three characteristics: First, after the emergence of the Internet, information has changed from being unconnected to being connected in high-dimensional space-time. Before the emergence of the Internet, all information was not connected to each other, and media communication activities were carried out in a linear way; after the emergence of the Internet, all information is freely connected in cyberspace, and an "ordered chaos" is formed. This chaos is caused by the fact that information in cyberspace transcends the boundaries of linear time. Secondly, after the network media downscale the information, the information is presented to the audience living in three-dimensional space and time with the characteristics of four-dimensionality, i.e., the information has the characteristics of transforming the chance into necessity within a certain range. Third, the network media has the function of bridging four-dimensional space-time and three-dimensional space-time, because the development and popularity of media technology, individuals have mastered the ability to freely downscale information according to their needs, enhance the ability to receive and release information, increase the frequency of information interaction, and ultimately, the total amount of information interaction has greatly increased, and the information explosion has resulted.[168]

---

[168] Dong Chao, Rules of information communication from the perspective of spatio-temporal dimension, Modern Communication, February 2018

II. Social media functionally has the role of building multiple information worlds

The concept of multiple audience information worlds is inspired by the hypothesis of multiple universes in quantum theory. The theoretical hypothesis of multiple universes is mainly based on consciousness and philosophy as a starting point, and the American physicist Hugh Everett proposed the interpretation of multiple worlds based on quantum theory. The rationale is that quantum theory suggests that a single event can produce multiple outcomes when it occurs, so there will be multiple universes. Later, through the interpretation of string theory and M-theory about "membranes", they believe that the universe we live in is a fragment of multiple "membranes" that are torn apart, so there are multiple worlds. According to the superstring theory, some scholars believe that there are many variations of space-time from ten to four dimensions, so there is a very rich universe in existence, and when this theory entered into the vision of philosophy of science, some scholars made a philosophical reflection on the multiverse. It should be emphasized here that the philosophical reflection of quantum theory applied to the study of information communication is using the results of such philosophical reflection to talk about information communication instead of describing it, and the multiverse view is a more convincing perspective for us to talk about the phenomenon of social media communication.

First, each audience has a separate world of interpretation. If social media communication is seen as a relationship between countless individuals making connections, each person is an independent individual, and although it may show convergence due to values, ethnicity, culture, religion, etc., each person is each person, and they are all independent and not exactly equal, just as philosophers say there are no two identical leaves, and there are no two identical people in the world. The differences referred to here do not refer to the differences in biological characteristics, but to the differences in the spiritual level, including the complex aspects of individual values, worldview and life view from macro to micro. Each person's difference creates a different interpretation of the world, and the world we speak of is the world as it is. The world that each person speaks about is also different, which is more obvious in real life, so each person is an independent individual with different consciousness, all using their own ideas to explain the world.

Second, each audience is doing information interaction with other people. From the moment a new life is born, the information interaction has begun until life stops. Of course there are biological scientists and doctors who say that the independent consciousness of an individual exists from the moment a new life becomes an embryo and grows brain nerves; we do not examine it in such a specific and subtle way. It can be clearly said that man has already begun to interact with the world when he becomes conscious, and from the time of birth he has to interact with the whole society, and this interaction includes direct contact with people and indirect contact with people, and for any life, in the final analysis, it is people who can interact and communicate with him. Through these interactions and the genetic consciousness brought by birth, life begins to generate interactions with the world, explaining and perfecting its own explanatory system, and information communication is an important link in the structure of this explanatory interaction.

Once again, individuals are experiencing the transformation of information communication from a linear structure to a three-dimensional structure. The above mentioned media is a change process, and this change process mainly follows the path of linear to three-dimensional communication transformation and centralized to decentralized communication transformation. In this process there are organized information communication media are reduced and personal information communication capacity is enhanced. Communication is ultimately the communication of people and people. Before the emergence of social media, this process was a unified collection of information and communication of information by centralized and organized media, and to borrow the words of Zhao Tingyang, the world is what the media says. After the emergence of social media, there is a trend of media integration, and "big" media and "small" media coexist, both of them are interactive information concentration, and the advantages of traditional media begin to be changed. Therefore, social media has changed the information communication between people from linear to three-dimensional, and from single to multiple, which is a process to make information communication convenient.

Finally, individuals build their own worlds in interaction through the information spoken in social media, and each person is an independent world of information. The world of personal information is built based on the mental world composed by the interaction between the individual and the world. Each person refines and enriches his or her personal information world in the interaction with the world due to the diversity of individuals, the diversity of media use and the irregularity of world changes. It can be said that for each different individual, he constructs an information world of his own. The point to be emphasized here is that social media play a role in accelerating and enriching the construction of this personal information world, which also existed during the traditional media in the past, just not so fast and rich. In the future, after the emergence of new media, such as 5G or even 6G, the speed of building the world of personal information will only be faster, richer in presentation and more diversified.

THE SCIENTIFIC-PHILOSOPHICAL EXPLANATION SYSTEM OF SOCIAL MEDIA COMMUNICATION

This paper argues that social media communication is based on human-to-human communication, and people have the objective conditions to build their own information world, and people are divided into consciousness and senses to view in the process of information communication, and information is interpreted as the symbolization of consciousness. As far as the communication process is concerned, it is based around two characteristics of information, one is the nature of information as a basic unit in communication, containing the superposition of symbols and consciousness, the correspondence between consciousness and bosons, and the other is based on the high-dimensional dimension in which the information itself is located and the three-dimensional linear relationship in time that the information must comply with in the process of communication. In terms of the understanding of social media itself, the function of social media is mainly manifested in the broader social information transmission, but also in the tool property of adjusting the spatio-temporal dimension of information, and at the same time in the establishment of the field of information communication through technology. From the perspective of the effect of social media communication, we can find that the "information quality" and the rate of information reaching, which is composed of the degree of participation of symbols and consciousness in the communication process, are the key to the communication effect. Therefore, this section is divided into two parts to explain how the scientific-philosophical concepts of uncertainty principle, probability theory, spatio-temporal dimension, and logic of association from information to people, from people to media, and from media to effect form an overall system. The second is to construct a symbolic and intuitive formula of communication effectiveness through "information quality" and "information dissemination rate" per unit of time.

I. The scientific-philosophical explanation system of social media communication

The previous discussion of this paper can be summarized in four aspects.

First, the assumption of consciousness communication in the form of information is the basis of the philosophy of science's explanation of social media communication. To some extent, information is an extension of consciousness, the senses are the natural extension tools after the extension of consciousness, and the media (including tools) are an extension of the senses. McLuhan was the earliest proponent of this idea, and this idea can be complemented and further explained in the present society as well. The direction of media development is to move from rough extension to precise extension, with the ultimate goal of unobstructed communication of consciousness and awareness. De-signification and de-mediatisation are trends driven by the origin of information. The subject of communication changes fundamentally, from human or human extension to consciousness communication, because the tool is the extension of human, the extension of human consciousness .

Secondly, the vision of "communication" needs to change, as long as one exists, communication exists naturally, and human beings are just chiseling through the tunnel of communication. Such thinking can explain not only all the validated theories of communication, but also the phenomena that are temporarily unexplained in communication research, as well as the phenomena that are completely ignored by communication science research. Consciousness and the spread of consciousness are natural. People and people, or people and people's consciousness, can spread beyond time and space, but we cannot observe it because of the objective barrier of three-dimensional space and time, that is, the barrier of linear time-based communication, which gives us the illusion that communication needs to be developed. The development of media technology is just breaking down the wall between consciousness and awareness, and technology has no role in changing the properties of information dissemination itself.

Third, the three-dimensional spatio-temporal reading limit also creates the law of audience attention conservation: every day a single individual in the information received because the time is fixed 24 hours, which is based on the insurmountable iron law of the current spatio-temporal state. We will find that in any topic, the core of the multiparty information release is intentionally or unintentionally competing for attention, even mobilizing audience emotions to trigger attention, with information relying on emotions and emotions constructed by facts to complete the storytelling. This is illustrated by the information communication of the Wuhan epidemic, where official, media organizations, and self-publishers took turns in releasing information that was competing for audience attention, while it can also be observed that using emotions, an objectively existing element of communication, is one of the more powerful weapons to compete for audience attention.

Fourth, in terms of social media itself, social media itself has two attributes, one is the attribute of being a tool for ascending and descending, and the other is the role of gas pedal with the development of technology. It can be said that social media is a spatio-temporal dimensional control tool with the ability to accelerate information communication. Accordingly, two practical roles of social media as a tool itself arise, one is to eliminate uncertainty, and it is widely accepted that some scholars believe that communication is something that eliminates uncertainty. As discussed earlier, the "information" in social media communication is uncertain, so eliminating uncertainty is the practical role of social media, and the theoretical tool to accomplish uncertainty elimination is the use of probability theory. The second is to improve the probability of the effect of information communication. Another practical meaning of social media is to improve the probability of effect of communication to accomplish uncertainty elimination. Quantum theory has a formula that represents probability: $d = F_n T_n$, where d represents the probability element, the formula expressed is the probability of occurrence at a certain moment, if we specify the probability of an event synthetically as 1, then many related events can be presented in mathematics as a normalized expression, $1 = d_1 + d_2 + d_3 \dots \dots d_n$, in which meaning, time comprise the main factors of probability change, so reducing uncertainty to increase the probability of communication is another practical meaning of social media communication. In the expression of these two formulas, we will also clearly find that the change of time is important, if extreme values of time are taken, it will have a huge impact on the effect of communication, so here we can make the time as well as the rate of information dissemination in time is a crucial factor, while so the change in the quantity of meaning and quality change is important. So in social media communication, the rate of communication, the quantity of information, and the meaning of information are three decisive factors.

II. The symbolic effectiveness formula of social media information dissemination: E=MhV2

If we take the information communication process as the research object, then the process must contain the following core elements: information, interaction rate, communication effect, and people (audience). In this paper, we stop the investigation of communication effect at "information arrival" for two reasons: First, the research method of this paper is a step-by-step study, which separates and then merges the absolute objective law and human subjective influence, i.e., we describe the absolute objective law first, then add human factors, and then try to reach the edge of the objective laws of communication research. Therefore, in terms of information communication effect, "information arrival" is the most objective and can be described and analyzed. Second, many theories that examine the effect of information communication activities between people have a common starting point, which is the arrival of information. Therefore, the most important issue that should be concerned about the effectiveness of information dissemination is "information arrival".

There are two clear criteria for judging information arrival, namely: "arrival rate" and "arrival information" (hereinafter referred to as "speed" and "information quantity"). At the objective level, the information dissemination effect (hereinafter referred to as "speed" and "information quantity") is the most important factor. At the objective level, the information dissemination effect (E) is equal to the product of information quality (M) and dissemination rate (V), because the dissemination necessarily involves two-way or multi-way, so the dissemination rate (V) needs to be squared. Re-entering the evidence above, the quantity of information, the meaning of information and the rate of information dissemination are important indicators of the elimination of uncertainty to improve the probability of communication effect, it is not difficult to derive the following symbolic formula.

In this way, the information propagation effect can be calculated by the following formula[169]which draws on Einstein's mass-energy equation $E=mc^2$, where E represents the energy contained in an object at rest, m represents its mass, and c represents the speed of light]. --E=MV2 This formula does not mean that the information dissemination effect has the ability to be calculated, but only expresses a force relationship in order to more clearly express the relationship between information dissemination effect, information quality and dissemination rate in the process of information dissemination. This formula shows that: the communication effect is proportional to the information quality, the greater the information quality (information quality refers to the degree of relevance of information to people), the better the communication effect; the communication effect is also proportional to the communication rate, the faster and more frequent the communication, the better the communication effect. The author believes that this formula has some explanatory power for all social media communication phenomena. In addition, if the quality of information is large enough, that is, the information is information that every individual in society urgently needs to obtain, then no matter how low the rate at which it proceeds, it will eventually reach the vast majority of individuals in human society, such as the Olympic Games and other major global events that people are generally concerned about and eager to learn about; conversely, no matter how irrelevant a message is to every member of human society, but as long as the rate of dissemination Conversely, no matter how irrelevant a message is to each member of human society, as long as it is disseminated fast enough and frequently enough, it can have a considerable influence on the majority of society members.[170]Therefore, this symbolic hypothetical formula of communication effectiveness is of some academic value when compared with the communication effects of social media.

---

[169] The formula draws on Einstein's mass-energy equation $E=mc^2$, where E represents the energy contained in an object at rest, m represents its mass, and c represents the speed of light.

[170] Dong Chao, Rules of information communication from the perspective of spatio-temporal dimension, Modern Communication, February 2018

CHAPTER 5

CASE ANALYSIS AND EXPLANATION TESTING IN SOCIAL MEDIA COMMUNICATION

Theory comes from practice, and guide practice. There is a famous line in Goethe's "Faust", which Lenin liked most and often quoted, "Theory is gray, but the tree of life is evergreen. In the Chinese dictionary, theory is "a system of concepts and principles, a rational understanding that has been systematized. A correct theory is a correct reflection of the essence and laws of objective things; it comes from social practice and guides people's practical activities". Therefore, we need to use some actual cases to explain and verify the theoretical overview of the characteristics of social media communication in the above study.

It is generally believed that social media came on the communication stage in the London subway bombing in 2005, after that, with the development of mobile broadband communication technology, 3G, 4G and 5G came into use one after another, the role and influence of social media became more and more important, especially in the communication of some major issues, take the U.S. election as an example, in the 2008 U.S. election, social media began to have "importance". It became "dominant" in the 2012 election and "decisive" in the 2016 election, with the extreme case of "social media triumphing over traditional media" as the opinion matrix constituted by mainstream media was unable to influence the election. In this paper, we have chosen the relatively new cases of the "British death van", the French" yellow vest movement" and the inappropriate comments of the NBA president (Murray case). In addition to the latest factor, the nature of the incident, the geographical factor, the intensity of the incident and the nature of Sino-foreign relations are also taken into account. The "British death van" is an incident that occurred outside of China and partially involved China, indirectly related to China, the French" yellow vest movement" is an international incident not related to China, and the "Moray incident" is directly related to China. The choice of these events mainly illustrates the global nature of communication, the fragmentation of information and the scientific-philosophical explanations presented behind them.

Social Media Presentation and Interpretation of the "British Death Van Incident"

I. Overview of the British death van incident

On October 23, 2019 at 1:30, a refrigerated container van was found in an industrial estate in Essex, southeast England, with 39 bodies hidden in the container van, causing the British government, the Chinese government, the Vietnamese government and the media of various countries to pay great attention to the case. On October 24 at 10:40 the British police informed the Chinese embassy that all those who died were suspected to be Chinese, at 11:01 the BBC Reported all the dead Chinese, 11:37 Essex police released an official statement, the dead are believed to be all Chinese nationality, October 25 BBC and the British Guardian reported that it is possible that six of them are Vietnamese nationality, the Guardian also cited an expert opinion claiming that Vietnamese to China and then smuggled to the United Kingdom, so may get Chinese nationality, November 1, Essex police statement that 39 people All Vietnamese, to November 7, 2019 Vietnamese public security department confirmed that the deceased are Vietnamese, November 8, together with the British police announced the list of the dead.

The focus of this story in China is that after the BBC released the news on October 24 that the 39 people who died were Chinese nationals, on October 25 China's Global Times and its editor-in-chief Hu Xijin both issued an article saying that the UK was responsible for the deaths of the "Chinese". 25 Chinese Foreign Ministry press conference, a CNN reporter asked a question, originally As follows: "Regarding the tragedy that occurred in the UK, we understand that there is limited detailed information available, but we would like you to provide some background. You mentioned earlier that in order to celebrate China's tremendous achievements and progress over the past 70 years, this month the junior high school held events related to the National Day. But Chinese citizens are leaving China through this extremely dangerous way, what are their motives? How should the outside world understand?" Hua Chunying replied to the other side's "preconceptions" and refuted them, and several Chinese official media followed up and issued comments, including an article on the Southern Weekend that CNN was eating buns of human blood.

II. the social media presentation and analysis of the "death van incident" in Britain

1. The media presentation of this event, in general, has received more attention from the media community and is a topical event in the short term. In this paper, the media coverage of this event is based on "British dead lorry", "British dead container", "British lorry tragedy", "British Essex lorry incident ", "UK truck corpse case", "UK container corpse case" as the theme words, searching in the main search sites, as of February 18, 2020, the data are as follows with " British dead lorry" as the keyword, Baidu has about 26,900,000 data, Google has about 8,530,000 data, Sina Weibo has about 419 data. With the keyword "British deadly container", Baidu has about 13,400,000 data, Google has about 2,310,000 data, and Sina Weibo has about 268 data. With the keyword "2019 UK truck tragedy", Baidu has about 9,760,000 data, Google has about 659,000 data, and Sina Weibo has about 8 data. With the keyword "Essex lorry incident", Baidu has about 30,700,000 data, Google has about 1,920,000 data, and Sina Weibo has about 81 data. The keyword "UK container tragedy" has about 1,270,000 data in Baidu, 348,000 data in Google, and 116 data in Sina Weibo. Baidu has about 12,500,000 data, Google has about 1,520,000 data and Sina Weibo has about 10 data for the keyword "UK truck body case". Using the keyword "UK container corpse case" as the keyword, Baidu has about 847,000 data, Google has about 518,000 data, and Sina Weibo has about 172 data.Based on Wikipedia, we compiled a total of 87 media and official releases that played a key role in the whole incident. The event was presented in social media, Sina Weibo for example from October 24 to November 9 with a total of 257 tweets, its official

CCTV news microblog in October 26 in the CCTV hot comment: "CNN owes 39 families of the victims an apology", which received more than 39 million plays, and many media reports of multiple days received different degree of attention, including more than 30 with more than 10 million VODs. The social opinion about the dead truck was completely ignited. As the country directly related to this incident is Vietnam, in the most social media, the keywords "39 people died in the UK" and "39 people died in the van" were typed in Vietnamese and searched on google, videos link and youtube. The search results on google showed 48,300,000 results, more than 60 video links with millions of hits, and 18 youtube search results with more than 1 million hits, which is not as hot as China's media response. Therefore, the overall media presentation pattern is that the Chinese public opinion environment is one of the main battlegrounds for the outbreak of public opinion on the event.

2. The reporting path of this event related to China. We can clearly see that the logic of the whole event is clear, 39 people were found dead in the truck in the UK, the official and local mainstream media released this event with China's relationship, the official British and BBC released on the 24th: "Chinese" stowaways died in the container, the Chinese government followed up the investigation, the official media CCTV, Global Times, Hu Xijin, etc. The official media CCTV, Global Times, Hu Xijin, etc. are the first time to speak out. The key information points "Chinese, death, stowaway", basically formed by these key words, this incident in the form of "personal insult" to Chinese people, and entered the field of Chinese public opinion, forming a large social opinion. It can be said that the incident itself is an official British "mistake", but when the truth is often not revealed, the first thing that ignites is the emotion that can cause public opinion.

3. The analysis of this event has the following characteristics. First, this event eventually proved to be in fact unrelated to China, but there is a greater connection in terms of information communication. The heat continues unabated, as shown in Chart 5.1.

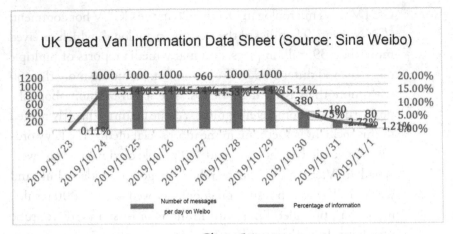

Chart 5.1

By examining the whole incident, we will find that this incident has nothing to do with China in fact, the transporting parties are not Chinese, the suspects are not Chinese, and the victims are not Chinese, but it has set off a larger public opinion concern in China. This shows that although facts are the basis of emotions, once the emotional field is formed in social media, then emotions are part of the reality. Second, this incident has the keyword of mobilizing emotions. Due to the police announcement and the BBC's early misleading report of Chinese official and Chinese media involvement in this news event, the main keywords for its communication are: illegal smuggling, Chinese, and death, which are all words with relevance to mobilize audience emotions. Finally, the truth of the incident, the media's voice, the government's statement, and public opinion were all in the midst of inaccurate information changes. Although the investigation of the incident was launched relatively quickly, the whole incident was investigated clearly after 15 days, and there is no time interval for social media communication, and timely information dissemination in the face of 15 days of investigation results, obviously the information "ran "in front of the facts. The result of the investigation is certain, but the process of the investigation is uncertain at the level of information communication, that is, from the perspective of social media communication, the information about the facts in the 15-day period is in a state of uncertainty. By the same token, media statements and government statements are all subject to greater uncertainty because they are in the process. During the period from October 23, 2019 to November 7, 2019, the investigation about the truth of the incident, the media speculation, and the emotional outpouring of public opinion are all ambiguous.

III. The explanation of the philosophy of science on the communication practice of "death van"

According to the characteristics summarized above, the main points to understand through the explanation of philosophy of science summarized in this paper are as follows.

First, the explanation of the third logic. The third logic pointed out in this paper is the logic of correlation. As we expressed before, there are two traditional logics in information communication, one is the logic of time and the other is the logic of event, and in the process of social media communication of this incident, we can clearly see the existence of the third logic. There is no direct factual connection between this incident, i.e. the person who transported the bodys was not Chinese, the person who died was not Chinese, the investigating party was not Chinese, and the countries involved in the incident did not include China, but such an incident made big waves from October 24 to November 9 from the Chinese government, Chinese official media, and Chinese civil opinion. The reason for this is the result of the forced information correlation between the unrelated events. The main focus is on two parts: the police briefing and announcement on the 24th, and the BBC report, which forcibly correlated the two countries and forced the Chinese audience into the public opinion field. As mentioned earlier, the focus of relevance is on emotional guidance. Emotions reflect a stronger bonding effect in the interpretation of events, and once an event mobilizes the audience's emotions, then it allows the information to have a correlation and aggregation effect. There is also a difference between strong and weak correlation in the correlation logic. The difference between strong and weak correlation lies in the degree of emotional correlation, which is expressed in the intensity of emotions of the participating audience, the number of participants, the existence of opinion leaders among the participants, and other factors. In this case, it is obvious from the number of related information and the frequency of participation that the public opinion field in China is the most "violent", because it is the public opinion field in China that has the highest emotion mobilized, so this event is a typical strong correlation.

Second, the importance of uncertainty in social media communication. We will find in the case of the British death van, the main reason that can contribute to the intense spread of this event also includes the uncertainty of the event and the uncertainty of the interpretation of the event, we know that communication is the elimination of uncertainty, this event in the most intense period of communication (October 24 - October 29), the truth of the event is uncertain, the media caliber is uncertain, the future direction of development is uncertain, basically from the "present" to the "future" is an uncertain state of change, the uncertainty of the event brings uncertainty of interpretation, especially the interpretation with emotion, which greatly increases the uncertainty of information in the process of social media communication. This uncertainty brings a great deal of imagination to the development of the event, and all parties involved interpret the event through their own will, so we can see through this case how important it is to reduce uncertainty and increase the accuracy of communication and finally to emphasize that this case can show that the biggest uncertainty comes from the double uncertainty of event and the communication report .

Finally, emotion is the most crucial communication driver. As explained in this paper, the information disseminated depends on emotions, and the interpretation of information depends on emotions, so it can be said that in this case the truth of the incident is the foundation, and the direction of social media communication depends on the rise and fall of emotions. The "ebb" and "flow" of emotions is the key to the spread of the whole "emotional field". The reason why an event completely unrelated to China can generate strong public opinion in the Chinese public opinion field,the truth of the incident is important, but the information released by the British officials and the BBC from the very beginning was the "hurricane" that mobilized the "rising tide" of Chinese social media opinion field. The official release of terms such as "Chinese, smuggling, and death" in an authoritative manner, and the stringing together of these individual terms and their interpretation, inspire a national emotion that cannot be insulted. We know that if we divide emotions by degree, the simplest criterion is the number of participants and the duration of participation, and national emotions are a collection of many participants and a relatively long duration of participation so that what seems to be unrelated events are actually mobilized national emotions. So when we can see the connection between emotion and uncertainty, we can see that the certainty of facts is the best way to stabilize emotion and the result of this event is that the "falling tide" in the Chinese social media opinion field also comes from the fact that the facts have come to light and the facts that generated the insulted emotion are gone, so the emotion is dissolved. Without the dissemination of emotion, it is just the release of information, so the public opinion is calmed down. Through this case, we can see the powerful role of emotions in the information. It can be said that in the process of social media communication, emotions play the role of bonding information, and the communication of emotional field is the main battlefield of social media communication and furthermore, in a certain perspective, emotions even determine the degree of social media communication.

Social media presentation and explanation of the French" yellow vest movement"

I. Overview of the French" yellow vest movement"

It started on November 17, 2018, and was directly triggered by the people's dissatisfaction with the government's fuel tax increase and took to the streets, which had a direct impact on many aspects of French politics and economy, and also affected the surrounding areas of France. The French" yellow vest movement" is the most intense and longest lasting riot in France in the past fifty years since World War II. The movement lasted for a long time, and the people had no fixed leadership team and no fixed demands, but it had a strong negative impact on the society. The French government has also made measures such as raising the minimum salary and reducing income tax on overtime in order to maintain the stability of the country. As of November 16, 2019, tens of thousands of people still participate in rallies and hold demonstrations. According to the British newspaper The Guardian, it is difficult to give a simple explanation to the French" yellow vest movement", which is not a holistic, focused and simple movement, it has no leadership structure and no single demand, which is why it is confusing and worrying.[171]

In this movement, information dissemination and mobilization showed different characteristics than before. The internal mobilization of the participants in the French" yellow vest movement" is characterized by a flattening of social media, a wider and faster range, and an accelerated diffusion of social movements. Charles Tilly argues that "the most significant role played by the new media over the course of the movement's

---

[171] John Lichfield. Just who are the gilets jaunes? [EB/OL] . （2019-02-09）[2019-02-16] . https://www. theguardian.com/world/2019/feb/09/who-really-are-the-gilets-jaunes.

long history is not so much in reshaping the movement's image in the media, but in connecting its actors to the media's intra-circular audience."[172]

II. The social media presentation and analysis of the "yellow vest movement in France"

Baidu has about 1,860,000 and Google has about 18,700,000 for the keyword "yellow vest movement in France". Baidu has about 12,000,000 and Google has about 10,300,000 keywords for "French yellow undershirt movement". The keyword "French riots" has about 9,980,000 data in Baidu, 6,390,000 data in Google, 521 data in Sina Weibo, and about 55 groups in Facebook dedicated to "Yellow vest ".From the perspective of population distribution, the British are more involved. There are 996 articles about the "yellow vest movement" on WeChat, in which the main topics are "Macron's political crisis", "violence, riots", "populism"and so on. The keyword "Yellow vest movement in France" has 6,120,000 entries in google, and the keyword "Yellow vest movement in France" has 6,120,000 entries in facebook. There are only 18 search results in Facebook for the keyword "Yellow vest", and more than 100,000 search results in Instagram for the keyword "Yellow vest". The number of search results in google for the keyword "Mouvement gilet jaune" is 3,160,000.

In the media presentation of the "yellow vest" movement in France, it can be found that the event is a typical international news event with low participation of media outside France and mainly official media in China, while social media has become a communication channel to shape the public opinion in France. In France, the Yellow Vests movement has become a "flat, democratic network of organizations in revolt against the power system of the political economy and the media elite".[173]In this movement, social media has become a means of communication and a self-organized information channel for the members of the "yellow vest" movement.

---

[172] Charles Tilly, Hu Weijun, Social Movements: 1768 - 2004, Shanghai, Shanghai People's Publishing House, 2009

[173] Sun Xingjie, Populism and the dilemma of French governance: an analysis based on the yellow vest movement, Studies in United Front Studies, March 2019

III. The explanation of the philosophy of science on the communication practice of French" yellow vest movement"

Through the above cases with more characteristic communication events, we can use part of the theoretical explanation of this paper to understand this communication phenomenon, the most important of which is the emotional interaction, which we found in our study that the search results through Weibo, WeChat, Zhihu and other platforms are 232. The above conclusion shows that the yellow vest movement was a hot news event that was followed globally, and the event was deeply reported in traditional media and also widely discussed in social media. The public opinion field of this time is "yellow vests", "French revolution", "government-population conflict" and other topics with strong political color. The public opinion field around this time is also different from the mainstream media (traditional TV, newspapers, radio, etc.) in social media.Once the topic entered the social media context, there was a strong change of topic, with the most accepted topics in social media being "Macron," "luxury goods," "vandalism," "women" and other less political topics.In addition, through the above data, we can see that emotional issues appear frequently in social media, traditional media channels such as "BBC NEWS", "CBS" and other traditional content providers in social media present hard content "quality", but less interactive topics, relatively speaking, in social media with "grassroots" characteristics of the self-publishing platform content "quality" and traditional media still have a certain gap, but due to the topic selection and other factors, its topic interactivity, spreadability are stronger.

Emotion, and emotional field become the main factors affecting social media communication. In social media communication, emotion is an important point of investigation when judging the communication ability of each self-media platform and self-media platform in social media. The ability of the content released by the platform to mobilize the audience's emotion is the communication ability of the platform. The emotion builds the emotional field and the value identification or value conflict caused by the emotional field is an important path for the social media communication effect, while the interpretation of the value conflict caused by the event conflict in social media becomes an important motive behind the influence of the communication effect, which is finally presented as the public opinion field around the emotional theme. It is worth noting that this public opinion field is not a static public opinion field, because the event lasts for a long time from the occurrence to the climax to the end, so it is still a flowing public opinion field, that is, as long as people who are concerned about this matter enter the public opinion field, they will participate in the information interaction with the ups and downs of the whole event, and it is easy to form their own "hard" emotional field due to different values.The interaction from personal information becomes the spread of "emotional field" based on values of multiple parties.From the very beginning of the street march, vandalism and robbery of luxury stores, a variety of themes around the French "yellow vest" movement, we can make an analogy, one after another event is like a "dry wood", again and again thrown into the "fire" of the burning emotional field encounter, so we can say, social media communication, awareness, emotion, scene is not only an important element of the new communication, but also the main "burning" power.

Social Media Presentation and Interpretation of the "NBA President's Inappropriate Comments" Incident

I. Overview of the "NBA president's inappropriate comments" incident

October 5, 2019 NBA Rockets manager Morey tweeted, "Fighting for freedom, walking with Hong Kong," causing high concern in the United States, China and others, CCTV, CCTV News (microblogging) issued a statement that on issues related to China's sovereignty, the attitude of CCTV sports channels is serious, distinct, consistent and there will be no ambiguity and no room for maneuvering. The incident was highly debated in the Chinese media. The same day Rockets owner Phil Tita tweeted that Morey does not represent the Rockets. 7 October 2019 Morey tweeted again: "My tweets represent only my personal views and in no way represent the NBA or the Rockets", tweeting that Chinese social media is once again hotly debated, saying they cannot accept this kind of rhetoric. October 8 NBA president Adam Xiaohua face the media when responding to Houston Rockets general manager Murray made improper remarks involving Hong Kong: "We support Murray." One stone has stirred up a thousand waves.The national media is becoming increasingly vocal in its crusade.NBA president Adam Xiaohua responded to Houston Rockets GM Murray's inappropriate comments involving Hong Kong, and on October 9, CCTV Sports, the central broadcasting station, decided to immediately suspend NBA broadcasts.CCTV's statement received 260,000 likes at the microblogging end, and CCTV also said by name: "NBA president Xiao Hua defended Murray with "freedom of speech", "Murray incident" in Chinese society does not have much to do with the so called 'Freedom of speech' .The more you take this reason to explain the more hypocritical it is". So far the NBA's insulting incident has become a highly publicized media event. Therefore inappropriate comments and media fermentation, after CCTV suspended the NBA broadcast, Xiao Hua and others went to China for crisis PR, but refused to admit the mistake, Chinese public opinion clamor for voice is still strong. This incident also brought huge losses to the NBA's revenue in China.

II. the social media presentation and analysis of the "NBA president's inappropriate comments" incident

Using "NBA president's inappropriate comments" as a keyword, Baidu has about 2,430,000 data, Google has about 2,000,000 data, People's Daily, CCTV News and Global Times posts 63 news articles on Sina Weibo from Oct. 6 to Oct. 19, with a total of 1,348,000 reads. Among them, CCTV issued 13 articles and Global Times issued 23 articles, all of which received high attention. It is important to emphasize that the search revealed that Warriors head coach Kerr and a small number of NBA players had also made inappropriate comments related to China, but none of them attracted so much attention.

Comparing with Facebook's data, during the period of October 5 to October 19, a key search of "NBA's insulting remarks" revealed that Deutsche Welle, International Morning Post, Radio France Internationale, Voice of America Chinese Network, BBC Chinese Network, etc. posted 13 articles, but the most number of likes received was 524, and the search results of Twitter were roughly the same.First of all, the nature of this incident is an international news event, because the news participants are international, but the media heat is more intense in the domestic media. Secondly, the coaches and players of the Warriors and Pelicans had a small number who posted articles "supporting" Morey's inappropriate comments at one time or after October 5, but they did not form a large-scale hot topic. The uncertainty of the effect of information dissemination is evident, and also reflects the relevance of the Rockets' position in the hearts of Chinese audiences compared to other teams, and being hurt feelings is easy to provoke the audience's emotions. Therefore, the media performance of this event is an international event that is cold outside and hot inside, and the core is that relevance and emotional choice together contribute to the uncertainty choice of information dissemination.

III. The explanation of the philosophy of science on the communication practice of the "NBA president's inappropriate comments" incident

The "NBA president's inappropriate comments" incident can be seen as a low-density public opinion field, in which all social media users are "consuming" this "information feast" In this case, and platforms such as Hu Pao and Baidu Post have opened special discussion zones, and several platforms such as Weibo have formed special discussion topics. From the point of view of communication explanation, it can be said to cover several important conclusions drawn in this paper, the previous article has focused on the proof will not repeat, I think there are two more important features can become the case to prove the point. One is the partial proof of the information downscaling function of social media, and the second is the personal information world explanation of individuals or organizations.

1. Social media has the function of information downscaling. This paper previously used theoretical reasoning to demonstrate that social media is a way to downscale high-dimensional information into the three-dimensional readable real world for reading. There are two features in this explanation.

First of all, around a theme, no matter how complicated and diversified the information is, no matter how much information there is, people have an extreme value of acceptance, a theme field is like a "vortex of information space and time", attracting all the relevant information to produce a huge information quality. The audience is overwhelmed when the focus of attention is constantly shifting. Using Occam's razor, we summarize this situation as the principle of "attention conservation", which generally means that people's attention is limited and the high attention to a certain topic inevitably dissipates the attention to other topics, as some scholars have argued in the early days of social media .At the beginning, based on empirical observation,It is found that the heat of a hot topic does not exceed seven days, and in recent years, the concept of "golden 72 hours" is proposed in the field of public opinion management, which means that the heat of a topic does not exceed three days, and recent studies show that there may be "golden 24 hours" for a topic. In other words, a topic's hotness will not exceed one day, and the change of a topic's hotness from seven days to one day in social media is attributed to the problem of information reception of a single topic. Assuming that the amount of information on a certain topic is set at 100%, the time for the audience to "digest" 100% of the information is seven days due to the limitations of technology, the limitations of communication methods and the frequency of other hot information outbreaks, etc. By the recent development of social media technology, social media communication channels are diversified and social media information productivity has increased.The production capacity of social media has increased, especially similar to this "NBA president's inappropriate comments" incident, the topic point is relatively single, Murray, Xiaohua continued to stimulate Chinese public opinion through Twitter, this stimulation has brought the Chinese social network values consistent interpretation, Chinese netizens' interpretation reflects the way including a variety of forms of content production, pictures, text, video, interactive, etc. Chinese netizens' interpretations are manifested in various forms of content production, including pictures, text, images, interactions, etc., and the interpretations are constantly self-produced in this particular cycle.So as the total number of topics continues to increase, making the audience read information more frequently and faster, the human attention to a single topic also creates the effect of rapidly shortening the reading time. So in the face of complex information, and the audience's conservation of attention (the maximum amount of information received is almost a fixed value), social media becomes a tool to downscale a large amount of information that does not exist linearly into something that can be read following a linear time. And what needs to be emphasized again here is that at the information level is the information vortex formed through social media, where high attention topics form a vortex of attraction that draws all relevant, captureable and presentable information to the topic.

Second, the "information space-time vortex" formed by the theme of social media communication. Social media's descending characteristics also directly affect the survival of self media. In the traditional media period, after a piece of information is spread and read according to the timeline, it is not very likely that it can be extracted, processed, spread and read arbitrarily and completely, but the current social media situation is that, with the development of media technology, as long as a piece of information is read and forms a hot spot, there will be all relevant information of information " publishing" platform will be constantly developed, not to do one by one example, in short, in social media communication, based on a theme and the real existence of the "information vortex", not only to increase the dissemination of information, but also to be able to bring the higher dimensional information past down to the "here and now" to be read again. This can also explain why many of the current self-publishing media once the content reserves of a certain topic, waiting for the explosion, and even become patient enough to wait, there will be an effect, because we generally see a flowing timeline, but the operation of social media has long been out of the timeline and existence, not because social media is three-dimensional linear, but because we can only see three-dimensional and linear, the way we read limits our understanding of social media.

2. The explanation of multiple "personal information worlds". Another feature of the "NBA president's inappropriate comments" incident in social media communication is the construction of a personal information world. There are two parts in it: first, it is a close combination of the real world and the virtual world. Earlier we borrowed the words of Mr. Zhao Tingyang, "The world we speak about, the world as it is." This event gave most people a sense of the near unity between the spoken world and the real world. The statements in support of Murray and Xiaohua in social media outside of China have formed a self-consistent world of nothingness under the guise of "freedom of speech". For the virtual world, it also includes the information world constructed by the facts provided by the information and the virtual world constructed by the interpretation of the information world.The world constructed in social media contains the world of information and the world of interpretation, and the audience interacts with the virtual world of information through cell phones, and the audience's sense of reality is largely replaced by the world of information, and the integration of the real world and the world of information has never been so profound, as one author said in a WeChat article, "I live in your world.Secondly, the personal information world is constructed by individual consciousness together with others. As shown in this paper, each person is an independent information world constructor, and each person selects information and forms the information world through his or her own independent consciousness, and in this process, the individual completes two actions, "refining the personal information world

awareness" and "repairing the personal information world", adhering to his or her own values while continuously improving and partially modifying the personal information world through social media dialogues with the world. We live in a world where the overwhelming amount of information brings about a very busy dialogue between individuals and the world. In this case, however, the "emotional field" in which the conversation can take place is single and "stubborn". Fast-flowing information is most likely to be selected by individuals who are in line with their own values, consciousness or emotional tendencies, and most people want to accept what they think is right, so most people are "perfecting the world of personal information. According to the principle of attention conservation, audiences have more information reading possibilities, so it is difficult to change their perception of a certain topic once it is formed, which must be influenced by basic values, etc. However, in terms of pure information interaction, it is the basic reading characteristic of audiences that they are not willing to accept more ideas but only information that conforms to their own values, and this incident also reflects the information vortex correctness under the stubborn idea. However, it is undeniable that this incident can be clearly explained for the "personal information world", that is, the audience talks to the noisy public opinion field through their personal consciousness, forming the personal information world, and then processes and disseminates this information through their personal consciousness, creating a world of personal information with as many different values as there are audiences in social media.

CHAPTER 6

FURTHER EXPLANATION AND REFLECTION ON THIS STUDY

The previous paper has mainly carried out the conceptual analysis, theoretical explanation and case test, the author in this chapter of this study proposed in the important concepts and main ideas to re-explain at the same time, this research paper of the shortcomings of further explanation, according to the results of this paper, a brief description of this study later research focus and difficulties. At the same time, the author of this paper is well aware that there are still many imperfections in this paper, which are presented here, only these can only be further compensated in the future research.

REORGANIZATION OF THE IMPORTANT CONCEPTS AND MAIN IDEAS OF THIS STUDY

Due to the complexity of this paper and the large number of concepts and ideas used, the following elaboration is made in order to make the style of the paper clearer. The author considers the concepts of "philosophy of science," "information," "consciousness," "uncertainty," "spatio-temporal dimension" and "symbolic formula of social media communication" are the six most important concepts in this paper, so they need to be further explained and clarified.

I. Reinterpretation of the philosophy of science used in this paper

As pointebd out in the introductory chapter, philosophy of science has at least two research directions from the point of view of conceptual translation, a philosophy of science and a science of philosophy. The latter is a reflection on the purpose, method, and object of philosophical research, on the ontology, epistemology, and methodology of philosophy, which is not suitable for the research needs of this paper. And the first kind is the philosophy of science, which means the philosophical reflection on the process and conclusion of scientific research, and the philosophical thinking abstracted from the process of scientific research. Since this paper is about the study of social media, which belongs to the scope of philosophy and social science with a wide academic coverage, this paper borrows the first research direction, that is, the philosophical explanation of science, hoping that the theory after the philosophical reflection of science can be useful to the field of news communication. In addition, it should be stated and emphasized that this paper does not directly adopt the results of natural science research as the theoretical basis, but uses the philosophical theories developed by philosophers of science through philosophical reflection on natural science as the starting point for interpretation. Therefore, the concepts and explanations used in this paper, such as uncertainty, probability, spatio-temporal dimensions, symbolic formulas, etc. are applied as a kind of philosophical reflection. Since quantum theory has entered the field of philosophy of science, these terms, which originally belonged to natural science, especially physics, have been introduced into the philosophical discourse. It can be said that the terminology of theoretical physics used here is not directly based on theoretical physics, but is introduced into the philosophy of science, mostly from the philosophical reflections of Reichenbach and others, and follows the usage habits of Reichenbach and others. Finally, as an additional note on this issue, one of the core concepts used in this paper is consciousness, and the process of eliciting this concept is a conceptual understanding formed by comparing the findings of the fields of consciousness research, including the fields of philosophy, social sciences, and biological sciences, and this paper adopts a fusion approach, ultimately choosing to stand on the basis of the research of brain neuroscientists such as Damasio and Gazzaniga, forming materialistic understanding of consciousness by applying the Marxist materialistic dialectic approach. Since the understanding of consciousness is based on the neuroscience of the brain, and the neuroscience of the brain is generally considered to be a field of natural science, it is in accordance with the scope of the study of the philosophy of science to think philosophically based on the field of naturoscience and to use its abstracted philosophical concepts, and the concepts cited are also cited from the philosophy of science, which is the only concept of philosophical reflection on the system of natural science outside of theoretical physics used in this paper. The above reinterpretation is made here.

II. The reinterpretation of the concept of information in the communication of social media

The concept of "information" examined in this paper includes the concepts of journalism and communication, computer field, especially information theory, and also the microscopic field of interaction information between microscopic particles, which is a philosophical reflection on physics, and the concept of "information as the symbolization of consciousness" is proposed after synthesis. This is because comparative studies have revealed that most of the knowledge of information exists in absolute objectivity, as well as most studies have not clearly described the structure of information itself, especially in the field of information communication. This is because comparative studies have found that most of the knowledge of information exists in absolute objectivity, as well as most studies have not clearly described the structure of information itself, especially in the field of information dissemination. The relationship between information and consciousness is more often considered to be juxtaposed or recursive, but the actual examination of information communication, especially social media communication, reveals the relative complexity of the relationship between information and consciousness. First, consciousness must be a part of information, which has been fully expressed in the introduction and chapter 1. Second, consciousness and information themselves are externally related, which means that if we look at consciousness as a whole concept, it is both contained and externally related to information, and the relationship between information and consciousness cannot be viewed from a single perspective. In addition, there is a reinterpretation of the existence dimension of information. The viewpoint of this paper is that information itself can exist in higher spatial and temporal dimensions, such as four-dimensional spacetime, which means that time is examined as a fixed quantity like length, width and height in space, and only in the process of propagation is information downscaled to the timeline for propagation so that the existence spacetime of information is an unknown high-dimensional spacetime, but the information in the process of propagation must exist in the three-dimensional space-time. Here we need to do some more extensions, which are about the storage and presentation of information. The existence of information, the storage of information and the presentation of information have a clear empirical logic, and the presentation of information depends on the storage capacity of information, especially on the quantity of information storage and the storage method, and the storage of information depends on the existence of information. It should be emphasized here that the storage of information only stores the part that can be symbolized under the premise of existing technology, and even only stores the information that can be presented that has been symbolized, not including the information that has not been symbolized and cannot be presented. It can be considered that with the development of media technology to develop new storage technology and presentation technology, it makes the original unexplored information have the possibility of being presented again.

III. Reinterpretation of the role of consciousness in social media communication

In the discussion of this paper, consciousness plays three central roles. First, in the composition of information, as the smallest unit of communication, consciousness is the core part of the composition of this smallest unit, similar to the boson in the smallest substance that makes up the material world, which does not occupy space, but is the glue of symbols and the basis for the embodiment of the uniqueness of information. At the same time, it is the basis for the spatio-temporal characteristics of the social media communication process because of its non-physical objective existence and its ability to transcend the spatio-temporal dimension. Second, the external characteristics of consciousness in the communication process, which refers to the consciousness of the other or the collection of the other's consciousness outside the message, these external consciousness has the ability to glue the information into the content of communication, and because the content of communication is generated by the symbolization of consciousness, so the examination of a single event can be understood as the field interaction of consciousness, and then because consciousness is the most important component of the determination of emotion, consciousness of the objective way of expression in the communication process is the emotional field, so the communication field composed of consciousness and emotion in the communication of social media is an objective and inevitable existence, so that the broader communication process can also be well understood, which is the emotional interaction between the field and the field is also the interaction between the field of consciousness and the field of consciousness. Third, the above analysis enables researchers to pay attention to consciousness and emotion as objective existence in the process of social media communication. In the process of social media communication, symbols, people, and communication tools all exist objectively, and even cultural, political, and economic reflections arising from the interaction of these specific objective things have become objects of objective examination and reflection and we have reasons to include consciousness and emotion in the new communication constituted by social media are included as objective elements to be examined, and the participation of emotion and consciousness in the process of information dissemination is not evaluated positively or negatively, they are just a neutral objective existence.

IV. Reinterpretation of Uncertainty in Social Media Communication

Generally we understand uncertainty mainly based on the plurality of structural elements composition and change complexity, because of the many and complex, so uncertainty, this uncertainty is mostly refers to unpredictability. We often say that the main effect of uncertainty is brought about by chance, which is based on the inevitability of the linear flow characteristics of time, and that causality is at work on the uncertainty of things. However, the philosophical interpretation based on quantum theory is different. The philosophical thinking of quantum mechanics considers uncertainty as a necessary certainty, and Reichenbach firmly believes that "the only thing that can be determined is uncertainty", and he deeply agrees with Heisenberg's argument of quantum uncertainty. Since the origin of uncertainty is based on the double-slit interference experiment in physics and the understanding of quanta, it is generally accepted in the philosophy of science that uncertainty exists as a necessary understanding. Therefore, in this paper, uncertainty is ontogenetic and has nothing to do with complexity and simplicity; it is not an uncertainty of too many variables that cannot be measured and whose structure cannot be accurately predicted, but an innate uncertainty. Therefore, in the understanding of social media it will be found that the uncertainty of social media communication is reflected in the unpredictable uncertainty of the communication process. Often researchers and practitioners are looking for a definitive approach, but are able to find that all seemingly accurate communication theories have large limitations and uncertainties, so on the surface of communication, the fundamental explanation of communication results should be based on uncertainty. On another level, uncertainty is reflected in the content and its results. We believe that the content of communication includes the content produced by the communicator and the content produced in the process of communication, and the content in the process of communication is the concept of encompassing content, especially in the process of communication in the field and the field, the reproduction of information content itself has uncertainty and cannot be measured or accurately described in the middle state. If we observe every information dissemination process, we will find that the content in the dissemination process and its possible effects have the characteristics that we can only talk about but not describe, moreover, we cannot accurately predict. Therefore, uncertainty is a fixed state, which involves all aspects of social media communication.

V. Reinterpretation of the spatio-temporal dimensional properties of social media

First, the concepts of dimension and spatio-temporal dimension should be clarified again. Dimension in natural science mostly refers to the direction of measurement, in philosophy and social science dimension mostly refers to the thinking angle, for example, one more dimension in social science research means one more thinking angle. The space-time dimension is borrowed from the concept of physics, and the dimension of our life is the three dimensions of space composed of length, width and height, the length, width and height referred to here are specific, measurable, with sufficient measuring equipment is measurable, not a changing amount, is a fixed amount.From the perspective of space-time, the world we live in is this three-dimensional space that changes in time. Of course, the assertion that "time is a group consensus that absolutely does not exist" has been excluded here, and the discussion here is about the way time exists. There are three ways of expressing the existence of time: one is that time exists objectively and flows; one is that time exists relatively and is measured by the speed of light; and one is that time can exist like length, width, and height. Since this paper has already explained the existence dimension of information and the information dimension in the process of propagation, that is, the information propagation of social media is the process of information transformation between high and low dimensions, and the theory of fixed existence of time is proposed, which mainly comes from the dimensional understanding of superstring theory in the late development of quantum mechanics, so the author chooses the philosophical thinking based on the superstring theory on dimensions and the way of time existence as the basis of the explanation social media dimensional transformation.

Second, there is a reinterpretation of the dimensional properties of social media. First, with the development of media technology, in terms of function, media is always in the development of elevated dimensionality, from paper media to network media to social media, the information leaps from the expression of words to the integration of multiple expressions, and the information connection changes from a single linear to multiple interactions, so the media in terms of function is constantly elevated dimensionality, second, the media properties from a single information media to pan-media change its fundamental driving force is the ascension of media dimension, the concept of media is also undergoing iterative changes, media before the emergence of the network are news and other specialized information communication platform, with the change of technology, a variety of APPs have also become a communication platform, in essence, including Taobao, Jingdong and other platforms are also specialized information downscaling tools.

VI. Reinterpretation of the symbolic characteristics of social media communication effectiveness formula

In this paper, we propose the symbolic effectiveness equation $E=MhV2$, mainly hoping to make the simplest expression of social media communication effectiveness, which is borrowed from the equation of theoretical physics, but does not have the arithmetic ability yet, and only stays at the symbolic equation stage. The symbolic equation is also common in the natural sciences, and this equation is only to illustrate the role of information quality and communication rate in determining the effectiveness of communication, so as to help us better understand the effectiveness of social media communication.

SOME SHORTCOMINGS IN THE STUDY OF THIS THESIS

There is no doubt that it is difficult to manage such a large topic in this paper, which requires not only great academic courage, but also strong academic ability and academic accumulation, and in the process of writing the paper, the author also felt the difficulty of being overwhelmed at times. There is also no doubt that there are many problems with this paper, and the following three aspects can be thought of at present.

I. The systemic nature of the view of the new communication understanding needs to be strengthened

Since the understanding of social media in this paper focuses on the new form of communication formed by the scene constructed by emotions from consciousness, this paper proposes a conclusion that the role of consciousness and emotions in social media communication needs to be understood objectively, and then proposes the idea that communication is generated by the interaction of emotional fields constructed by multiple consciousnesses, and the possibility of releasing personal consciousness communication due to the advancement of media technology.Therefore, the assumptions of "multiple information worlds" and "conservation of attention" in communication are made, and the overall explanation of social media communication is based on the uncertainty principle of causal elimination and spatio-temporal dimensional migration. A further abstraction is the quantum discontinuity and entanglement based on causal elimination and spatio-temporal dimensional migration, which is summarized in the symbolic equation $E=MhV2$. This system appears to have an intrinsically self-consistent system from the composition of microscopic information, the propagation force of information to the propagation process to the propagation results, but in fact the logical self-consistency of this system has a large instability.

First of all, in terms of macro logic, it is doubtful whether the two contradictory logics can prove each other by using the linear logic of traditional experience to argue for the non-linear logic of non-traditional experience. At the same time, it is also doubtful to reason about the explanatory power of the value judgment of social media communication through these two logics, after all, Hume and others deduced the assertion that "the logic of necessity cannot be deduced from the logic of yes. Although this reasoning is based on the fact of existence itself, it is only a facal of reality that cannot be avoided by empirical observation to draw theoretical conclusions. As Heidegger argues, "the here and now is, and within certain limits always is, to apprehend itself from this interpretation of the here and now".[174]Also the appropriateness of adding nonlinear time to the understanding of information and media communication is an important point of doubt in this study. "The proof of the meaning of temporality for this existence is also tested by this explanation.[175]"If social media communication is considered as a whole, the linear flow of time is the basis for proving the existence of social media itself, while if the recognition of nonlinear time is added, then the recognition of social media should become that is linear time and nonlinear time are the two bases.

Secondly, from the point of view of the studied explanatory view, there is a lack of a more unified penetration, such as information is an independent energy unit, which has some explanatory power from the point of view of the independence embodied in the explanation of information and communication process, especially in the aspect of the common role of emotions composed by consciousness in the communication process. The association logic of two information units in the process of social media communication is based on the fact that information is a fixed unit, while the association is made through consciousness and emotional field, using the philosophical thinking of quantum entanglement, but the information as an independent unit is slightly insufficient and has obvious lack of explanatory arguments in terms of communication effects. In addition to the temporal logic and event logic, this paper proposes that

---

[174] Martin Heidegger, Chen Jiaying and Wang Qingjie, proofread by Xiong Wei, revised by Chen Jiaying, Being and Time, Life, Reading, New Knowledge,Xinzhi Sanlian Bookstore, September 2014, reprinted January 2019, p. 24
[175] Martin Heidegger, Chen Jiaying and Wang Qingjie, proofread by Xiong Wei, revised by Chen Jiaying, Being and Time, Life, Reading, New Knowledge,Xinzhi Sanlian Bookstore, September 2014, reprinted January 2019, p. 24

there is a third logic of correlation in social media communication, which is also mainly focused on the explanation of the information itself and the communication process, and lacks unity. At the same time, the internal logic of several explanatory views also lacks unity, uncertainty, probability theory, association logic, and spatio-temporal dimension explanation, all of which have the strength of not being able to unify into one explanatory system, with a sense of lack of unity.

II. Refinement and clarification of the type description of the research object

Another area for improvement in this paper is the lack of refinement of the research object. Since this study concentrates on the macro description and explanation of social media, the research object includes two large objects, the reality level and the theoretical level. In the reality level, not only the information producers, communication process, communication effect and media itself in the communication process should be examined, but also the relationship between information awareness and body, the relationship between awareness and content, the relationship between content and content and other multiple levels, and in the theoretical level, the theory of this discipline and the theory of social discipline, as well as other interdisciplinary theoretical systems related to it should be examined. It can be seen that the research object presents diversity and complexity while also reflecting unity. The observations of the research object in this paper have a large deficiency in the actual research.

First of all, the theoretical collection and analysis ability is insufficient under the perspective of theory as the research object. The original purpose of this study is to establish an explanatory hypothesis system, so it needs to do a systematic sorting of existing theories. This paper has done a longer sorting of existing theories by searching and classifying Chinese textbooks, Chinese monographs, Chinese papers, etc. However, due to the level limitation, the involvement in English monographs and articles only stays in those that have been translated, and a part of the more well-known but untranslated works and articles,so the theoretical literature search and crawl is not ideal and not fully achieved to fully grasp.A further regret is that a total of 163 relatively well-known, important and explanatory news communication theories have been sorted out, i.e. covering both macro and micro theories, both practical and critical theories, but the ability to systematically analyze, judge and even evaluate these theories is indeed somewhat reluctant, and only key theories can be selected for analysis, judgment and evaluation, and inevitably there will be omissions, and this part needs to be improved and strengthened.Therefore, in terms of the degree of grasp of the research object, it does not really cover everything. In addition, there are also major shortcomings in the analysis, one is that the author's education is limited, and I am afraid that there is a lack of understanding of the relevant theories as the object of study, and at the same time, because I do not have a systematic background in Western education, and most of the Western theories have strong characteristics of continuity and inheritance, so when doing the analysis, there may be some understanding is not in place, and the study may not be in-depth.

Second, the perspective of practice as the research object, the case and analysis ability is not enough. This text, for example, as the title indicates, is a global social media practice as the research object, in the impossibility of exhaustive media practice research, this paper in the case selection of thinking is two points, the first point is itself established is a set of theoretical interpretation system, so this set of analysis system, if established, then for the explanation of macro communication practice and micro communication practice should have some explanatory power. The second point is the representativeness, the object of global social media research is the event with global social media communication ability, and it should be significant, representative and scientific research. The three cases selected in this paper have such characteristics.Of course, it should be emphasized here that the selection of these three cases in this paper does not mean that only these three cases are the most suitable, there are many other cases that are suitable, it is that these three cases generally have the ability to illustrate in the communication process and can be used to see the big picture in a small way. In the use of practice cases, there are also regrets, for example, for data mining and collation, the method used in this paper is a combination of crawler and manual, in WeChat, microblogging, Twitter, Facebook and other important social media sites for the search and data collation of relevant topics, and will be representative of the practice of separate collation and data statistics, in the research method is actually a typical sample sampling analysis based on big data, with a certain illustrative nature, but does have room for deeper excavation and refinement.

III. The professionalism of the case study methodology needs to be improved

In the argument part of the essay, I hope that theory can be combined with practice, so I have chosen three cases as the proof of the argument. There are three shortcomings in the case study that need to be improved and perfected in the future study and research, firstly, the selection of cases can be more illustrative, such as the Hong Kong amendment fiasco, which can find a more suitable minor theme as the focus of the argument and secondly, there is still a big shortage in the use of case data and charts, there is always a sense of powerlessness that the data is very large and the analysis cannot keep up and cannot use the data and cases effectively, and a large amount of data remains unused after the paper is written.

DIRECTIONS AND POSSIBILITIES FOR FURTHER RESEARCH

The understanding of the problem is also the direction of our further research to be done in the future, mainly on three different levels.

I. Micro level

The micro level is to further systematize and refine the ideas and concepts derived from this paper through a large number of case studies. As mentioned in this chapter, there is still much space for refinement of the concepts and ideas derived from this paper. The main concepts that need to be refined in future research are the refinement of the concepts of information and consciousness, and the refinement of the relationship between consciousness and emotion.

First, the concept of the information presented in this paper needs to be refined again in the future. In particular, we should pay attention to three aspects: first, we should make a more complete conceptual examination, try to exhaust the existing research results, especially the excellent research results in related cross-cutting fields, pay attention to the latest research results in philosophy and brain neuroscience in the study of consciousness, study the relevance and independence of the study of consciousness thoroughly, and complete the definition of information in the context of philosophical thinking in physics. The second is the study of symbols, this paper has less discussion on symbols, on the one hand, because symbols have a conventional cognition in information dissemination, on the other hand, this paper does not involve the deep level of symbol research, of course, the author does not ignore the value of semiotics as a sophisticated discipline at all, just that the understanding of symbols in this study can use conventional cognition, but in the future direction of research, the relationship between symbols and consciousness can be done through the previous research to think more deeply. The third aspect is the study of the relationship between information and communication processes, especially the relationship between information and the spatio-temporal dimension. This clever relationship with the advantage of changing structure is an important bridge and link to systematize the relationship between information and communication.

Second, the relationship between consciousness and emotion needs to be refined in future research. Although this paper has discussed the correlation between consciousness and emotion in a relatively rough way, there is still room for refinement when it comes down to how it works at a refined structural level. Consciousness and emotion are, from a brain neuroscience perspective, manifestations of behavior and consciousness, and emotion can only be expressed in terms of behavior, but brain neuroscience findings have also repeatedly emphasized that having behavior is not the same as having consciousness, which also suggests that measuring consciousness through behavior has an inherent uncertainty. In our study, we found that the only way to measure emotion is through behavior, but since consciousness is hidden in behavior, the measured behavior is not the entirety of consciousness, so new breakthroughs are needed in the study of consciousness and emotion. In addition, this paper views social media communication as the interaction between the emotional field and the emotional field. The interaction mechanism, the interaction paradigm, and how the propagation power of information is reflected will be the direction of future research.

II. Meso level

The meso level is to refine the hypotheses that are yet to be tested. The hypotheses proposed in this paper are the hypothesis of the spatio-temporal dimension of information dissemination, the hypothesis of the conservation of attention, and the hypothesis of the third logic. These scientific-philosophical explanations based on global social media communication research are still in the hypothesis stage, and the truth or falsity of the explanations are yet to be tested by scientific research and practice.

First, the assumption of the spatio-temporal dimension of information dissemination requires theoretical discussions in philosophy of science and practical development of reconceptualization to discern the truth. It is the most important assumption of this paper that information exists in a higher dimension and the role of social media is to downscale information.

The direction of future research requires experimental proof of the spatio-temporal dimension of information, not only to prove the possibility of the existence of consciousness out of linear time, but also, and most importantly, to prove whether information that existed before but was not recorded can be reproduced again, and whether information that existed before but was not discovered can be reconnected and reinterpreted according to consciousness, If it can be proved that the existence of information can be re-symbolized, then the knowledge of information is solid and true, and the problem of spatio-temporal dimension will be a true proposition.

Secondly, the hypothesis of attention conservation proposed in this paper is not original, but has been studied by scholars in the political economy of communication, which is mainly used to criticize cultural imperialism and consumer society, to the effect that the audience's time and attention are treated as a kind of capital, which will not be expanded too much due to the limitation of the scope of this paper, this paper is concerned with the time and space dimensions, so the core of this hypothesis is to find the common property of all audiences based on the objective existence in the current spatio-temporal dimension, which is why it is proposed that in social media communication, the measure of mobile time is the only yardstick in the linear spatio-temporal space, and each person has only twenty-four hours, so if we look for a standard that must be conserved, then the audience's attention is conserved in the twenty-four-hour range. This hypothesis needs to be constantly falsified in future research, just like the popular way of thinking in the philosophy of science in the last century, science cannot be confirmed but only falsified, and this hypothesis can only be refined into a theoretical explanation in the process of constant falsification.

Finally, this paper proposes the hypothesis of association logic of social media communication, that is, the third logic hypothesis, which is based on the third logic other than temporal logic and event logic in social media communication. The biggest discussable space of this hypothesis may be to use empirical logic to deduce non-empirical logic. There are many similarities between association logic and event logic in comparison, but event logic follows the causal relationship of event certainty, or because the result goes to find the direct or indirect influencing factors with causal relationship. The association logic assumed in this paper refers to the association in the spatio-temporal dimension, which contains temporal logic and event logic, and this logical relationship is downscaled to the linear flow of spacetime, which presents is event logic and time logic, but many non-time logic and non-event logic communication phenomena appear in social media communication can only be explained by association logic. The difficulty point of this hypothesis is two, one is the theoretical derivation is a bit rough, not fine enough, the second is the need to find a large number of cases to argue, looking for a too superposition of theoretical derivation, "state superposition is not a potpourri, but a combination of probabilistic elements,following a clear and elegant set of mathematical principles."[176]Therefore, the subsequent research needs to find cases and refine the theoretical derivation together with scholars related to philosophy of science and communication.

III. Macro level

At the macro level, a simplified and systematic explanation of interdisciplinary writing is needed.

Although Einstein believed that "God rolls the dice not only in quantum mechanics and nonlinear dynamics, but also in fundamental number theory."[177]He has been trying to establish a unified explanation with determinism. The author is also well aware of the difficulty of finding a unified field-theoretic explanation of social media communication, but it is undeniable that we can simplify the results of the studies already conducted under the existing conditions to increase the vitality of this explanation. Therefore, future research needs to be interdisciplinary, including scholars from mathematics, theoretical physics, brain neuroscience, philosophy of science, and other disciplines. There are mainly experiments and arguments about the spatio-temporal dimension, experiments and arguments

---

[176] James Gleick, A Brief History of Information, People's Post and Telecommunications Publishing House, August 2018, p.358

[177] Foreword to Cristian S. Calude, Information and Randomness:An Algorithmic Perspective Berlin:Springer,2002),viii.P348, cited in, [US] James Gray K., A Brief History of Information, People's Post and Telecommunications Publishing House, December 2013, first edition (16th printing, August 2018) P337

about the role of the consciousness-body relationship in social media communication, thoughts and studies about how quantum theory can be combined with communication science, and equations about how to make the efficacy of social media communication computationally feasible, etc. It can be a long way to go.

REFERENCES

1. Lin Zhida,Research on the basic theory of communication. Southwest Jiaotong University Press, 1994
2. [US] Severin Tancard et al. Origin, Methods and Applications of Communication Theory. Huaxia Publishing House, 2000
3. [UK]Nick Stevenson. Understanding Media Culture. Business Press, 2001
4. Dai Yuanguang. Theory and Methodology of Communication Research. Fudan University Press, 2003
5. Li Mingwei. Survival of those who know the media, Beijing University Press, 2010
6. Duan Peng. Foundations of Communication: History, Framework and Extension.
   Communication University of China, 2006
7. Hu Yiqing, ed. Handbook of Western Communication Academic History. Beijing University Press, 2015
8. [US] Rogers. History of Communication. Shanghai Translation Press, 2006
9. [U.S.] Hyrum Lowry/Melvin DeFleur. Milestones in the Study of Mass Communication. People's University of China Press, 2003
10. [Canada] Innis. The bias of communication. People's University of China Press, 2003
11. [Canada] Marshall McLuhan. Understanding Media. Translating Lin Publishing House, 2011
12. [Canada] Harold Innes. The Bias of Communication. People's University of China Press. 2009

13. [US] Antonio Damasio. Descartes' error. Beijing United Publishing Company. 2018
14. Zhao Yifan. Lectures on Western Literature Continued. Sanlian Bookstore. 2009
15. Chen Shengsheng. The Concept of Communication. People's Publishing House, 2008
16. Zhang Yonghua. Media Analysis: Interpreting the Myth of Communication Technology. Fudan University Press, 2002
17. [English] Anthony Giddens. The Consequences of Modernity. Translating Forest Press, 2014
18. [US] Jeffrey Gorham. The philosophy of science that everyone should know. Zhejiang People's Publishing House. 2019
19. Hu Yong, Wang Junxiu, eds. After connection: public space reconstruction and power redistribution. People's Post and Telecommunications Publishing House, 2017
20. [US] James Gleick. A Brief History of Information. People's Post and Telecommunications Publishing House, 2013
21. Craig Callender/Nick Hergatt, eds. Physics and Philosophy Meet in the Planck Scale, translated by Li Hongjie, Hunan Science and Technology Press, 2013
22. Deyich. The Pulse of the Real World. Translated by Liang Yan and Huang Xiong. Guangxi Normal University Press. 2002
23. Yang Jianye. Yang Z.N. Biography. Sanlian Bookstore. 2016
24. Wu Guolin. Quantum philosophy of technology. South China University of Technology Press.2016
25. B. Green. The strings of the universe. Translated by Li Yong, Hunan Science and Technology Press. 2002
26. [UK] W.C Dampier. History of science. Translated by Li Heng. People's University of China Press. 2017
27. Chen Lidan. The impact of new media on social structure[J]. Democracy and Science,2013,(06):17-22.
28. Chen Lidan,Ding Wenfeng,Hu Tianyuan. Immersive communication:everywhere is the center and nowhere is the edge--summary and reflection on the World Internet Conference[J]. News Lovers,2015,(01):5-8.

29. Chen Lidan,Shi Wenjing. Analysis of the characteristics of Internet buzzwords[J]. People's Forum,2013,(18):64-65.

30. Peng Lan. Scene:the new element of media in the mobile era[J]. News reporter,2015,(03):20-27.

31. Hu Yicheng. Communication Technology and Civilizational Change: The Eternal Mother Tongue of Communication Studies - Reflections on the Innovation of Communication Discipline[J]. Journalism and Communication Research, 2007,(01):27-29.

32. Sun Xupei. New Achievements in Communication Science--Sense of Reading "Research on the Basic Theory of Communication Science"[J]. Journalism, 1995,(03):64.

33. Duan Jingsu. Basic Research in Communication and the Vitality of the Discipline[J]. International Journalism, 2009,(01):28-32.

34. Hu Yiqing. Behind the myth of the four founding fathers of communication science[J]. International Journalism, 2007,(04):5-9.

35. Peng Lan. From "mass portal" to "personal portal"--a key change of online communication model[J]. International Journalism, 2012,(10):6-14.

36. Peng Lan. From the old three networks convergence to the new three networks convergence: the redirection of three networks convergence driven by new technology[J]. International Journalism,2014,(12):130-148.

37. Peng Lan. From online media to online society--The gradual progress and expansion of China's Internet in 20 years[J]. Journalist,2014,(04):15-21.

38. Li Bin. Reflections and suggestions on research methods of journalism history[J]. Journalism University, 1996,(04):36-38.

39. Liu Xiaoying. The Historical Staging and Research Topics of International Journalism History[J]. Modern Communication, 2005,(02):36-40.

40. Mo Zhihong. Coase's theorem, personality rationality and economic efficiency: a restatement of Coase's theorem[J]. Research in Institutional Economics,2008,(02):46-57.

41. Cheng Chengping. Understanding Coase's theorem[J]. Academic Monthly,2009,(04):55-61.

42. Bian Donglei,Zhang Xiying. The Coming of Media Time: A Study on the Origin, Formation and Characteristics of the Concept of Time Shaped by Communication Media[J]. Journalism and Communication Research, 2006,(01):32-44+95.

43. Shao Peiren, Huang Qing. Media time theory: A study of the concept of media time[J]. Contemporary Communication, 2009,(03):21-24.

44. Peng Lan. Three types of media literacy and their relationship in the age of social media[J]. Journal of Shanghai Normal University (Philosophy and Social Science Edition), 2013,(03):52-60.

45. Bian Donglei. The New "Crossroads": Time Research in Communication and its Ideal Realm [J]. Journal of Nanjing University of Posts and Telecommunications (Social Science Edition), 2008,(03):48-55.

46. Peng Lan. The redefinition of news production under the trend of mobile and intelligent technology[J]. Journalist,2016,(01):26-33.

47. Li Xinren. Re-discussing spiritual interaction:Marxist view of communication and the reconfiguration of communication science[J]. Modern Communication (Journal of Communication University of China),2016,(08):19-23.

48. Lin Zhida. Emphasis on the basic theoretical research of communication [J]. Journalism University,1994,(03):13-16.

49. Li Bin, Cao Shule. A review of theoretical research on communication in China in 2006[J]. International Journalism,2007,(01):11-15.

50. Li Bin. Marx is back[J]. News Lovers,2013,(11):60-63.

51. Wu, Guolin. Transcendence and quantum interpretation [J]. Chinese Social Sciences, 2019, (2): 38-48.

52. Gao C, Qiao Xiaofei. The ontological connotation of duality in physics and its significance [J]. Nature Dialectics Letters. 2018

53. Ma N. Sense of screaming [M]. Beijing University of Technology Press.2016

54. Peng Lan. Introduction to network communication [M]. People's University of China Press. 2017

55. Wu Satisfaction. Introduction to network media [M]. National Defense Industry Press. 2007

56. ﹑Zhu Haisong. The fifth media [M]. Guangdong Economic Publishing House. 2005

57. Liu Ji. Research on the popularization and dissemination of contemporary Chinese Marxism in the network situation [M]. China Literature and History Publishing House. 2014

58. Sun Shaoyi. New media and cultural transformation [M]. Shanghai Sanlian Bookstore. 2013

59. Bao Ran. New Media [M]. Communication University of China Press. 2010

60. Liu Xiaohua. Internet + new media [M]. China Economic Press. 2016

61. Zhao Z. L. Introduction to network communication [M]. Sichuan People's Publishing House. 2009.

62. Shen Jinxia. Citizen Journalism in the Age of Self-Media [M]. China Radio and Television Publishing House. 2013

63. Zhou Xibing. Internetization [M]. Zhejiang University Press. 2016

64. [US] Nicola Negroponte. Digital survival [M]. Hainan Publishing House. 1996

65. Lin Xun. New media art [M]. Shanghai Jiaotong University Press. 2010

66. Du Junfei. Introduction to network communication [M]. Fujian People's Publishing House. 2004

67. Wang Gengnian. New media international communication research [M]. China International Broadcasting Press. 2012

68. Su Hongyuan. Introduction to Network Communication [M]. China Social Science Publishing House. 2010

69. [US] Alvin Toffler. The Third Wave [M]. Xinhua Publishing House. 1996

70. Li Liwei. Insight into "Internet+" [M]. People's Post and Telecommunications Publishing House. 2016

71. Xue Jinfu. Internet+ [M]. China Economic Press. 2015

72. Li Yihao. Internet+ [M]. China Fortune Publishing House. 2015

73. , Liu Chang. The communication logic of Internet thinking [M]. Communication University of China Press. 2015

74. Xie Weigeng. New media and society [M]. Social Science Literature Press. 2014

75. Xu Qin. Media convergence [M]. Communication University of China Press. 2009

76. [US] Jenkins. Convergence Culture [M]. The Commercial Press. 2011

77. Meyer Schönberg. The era of big data [M]. Zhejiang People's Publishing House. 2012

78. Cao Jin. Introduction to network language communication [M]. Tsinghua University Press. 2012

79. [E] McGuire. Mass communication model theory [M]. Shanghai Translation Press. 2007

80. Li Yanhong. Intelligent Revolution [M]. CITIC Press.2017

81. Wang F. The Great Media Convergence [M]. Nanfang Daily Press. 2007.

82. Chao Nai-Peng. China Network Communication Research [M]. Zhejiang University Press. 2011

83. Wang Qiu. Strategic transformation of broadcasting in the new media environment [M]. China Radio, Film and Television Press. 2015

84. Guo Xiaoping. Introduction to audiovisual new media [M]. Beijing University Press. 2014

85. Li Huaizhi. Introduction to New Media [M]. Xi'an Jiaotong University Press. 2015

86. Wang Yi. WeChat marketing and operation [M]. Mechanical Industry Press. 2013

87. [US] Marcia Redden Turner. The Godfather of New Media [M]. Machinery industry publishing house. 2002

88. Gao Shukai. The international media industry in the era of media convergence [M]. People's Daily Publishing House. 2012

89. [US] Paul Levinson. Digital McLuhan [M]. Social Science Literature Press. 2001

90. Cheng Yucheng. New Media Technology Theory [M]. Suzhou University Press. 2005

91. Gong Chengbo. Introduction to New Media [M]. China Radio and Television Press. 2007

92. Shen Qiwu. Research on the innovation and development of broadcasting in the new media era [M]. Jinan University Press. 2017

93. Xiao Yong. Winning in new media [M]. Oriental Publishing House. 2007

94. Zhong Ying. Network Communication Ethics [M]. Tsinghua University Press. 2005

95. Huang Shengmin et al. China's Broadcasting Media in the Digital Era [M]. China Light Industry Press. 2003.

96. [E]Joyson. Psychology of network behavior [M]. The Commercial Press. 2010

97. Gao Lihua. New Media Advertising [M]. Beijing Jiaotong University Press. 2011

98. Duan Yongzhao. Internet [M]. CITIC Press. 2009

99. Xiao Zanjun. Integration, Competition and Regulation in the Western Media Industry [M]. China Book Publishing House. 2011

100. Fu Xiaoguang. Media integration under Internet thinking [M]. Communication University of China Press. 2017

101. Hu Zhengrong. Television news innovation in the era of media convergence [M]. Communication University of China Press. 2011.

102. ﹨Cai Wen. Media convergence and convergent journalism [M]. People's Publishing House. 2012

103. Guo Yabing et al. China Digital New Media Development Report [M]. Communication University of China Press. 2006

104. Peng Lan. Frontiers of New Media Communication Research in China [M]. People's University of China Press. 2009.

105. [US] Schramm. Introduction to Communication [M]. People's University of China Press. 2010

106. Tencent Media Research Institute. The era of mass media [M]. China CITIC Press. 2016

107. Zhong Zhiyuan. Network Journalism [M]. Beijing University Press. 2002

108. Cui Baoguo, Li Kun. McGuire's theory of mass communication [M]. Tsinghua University Press. 2006

109. Ma Yunxia. Research on ideological and political education in colleges and universities in the era of "Internet+" [M]. People's Daily Publishing House. 2017

110. Wu Xinxun. New media and media economy [M]. Shanghai Sanlian Bookstore. 2008

111. Xie Xinzhou. Theory and practice of network communication [M]. Beijing University Press. 2004

112. Wu Bofan. The Carnival of Solitude [M]. People's University of China Press. 1998

113. Wu Feng. Network Communication [M]. China Radio and Television Press. 2004

114. Journal of Library and Intelligence Work. Research and dissemination of network public opinion in the new media environment [M]. Ocean Press. 2014

115. [E]] Chadwick. The Politics of the Internet [M]. Huaxia Publishing House. 2010

116. Deng Yu. Media convergence and freedom of expression [M]. Communication University of China Press. 2010

117. Huang Shengmin. The Mediaization Strategy of the Internet [M]. China Market Press. 2012

118. Min Dahong. Outline of Digital Media [M]. Fudan University Press. 2003

119. The Institute of Advertisers, Communication University of China. New Media Radical Change [M]. CITIC Press. 2008

120. Zhang Zhaozhong. Winning the information war [M]. World Knowledge Press. 2004

121. Shao Peng. News production in the context of media integration [M]. Zhejiang University of Commerce and Industry Press. 2013

122. Xiong Chengyu. New media and innovative thinking [M]. Tsinghua University Press. 2001

123. Tang Chaojing. Information theory and coding foundation [M]. Electronic Industry Publishing House. 2015

124. Tang S. W. Information theory [M]. Harbin Engineering University Press. 2008

125. Chen Hanwu. A concise tutorial on quantum information and quantum computing [M]. Southeast University Press. 2006.

126. Zhang Shujing, Qi Lixin. Information Theory and Information Transmission [M]. Beijing Jiaotong University Press. 2005.

127. Michael A. Nielsen, Isaac L. Chuang. Quantum computing and quantum information [M]. Tsinghua University Press.2004

128. Chen Zonghai,Dong Dao Yi,Zhang Chen Bin. Introduction to quantum control [M]. University of Science and Technology of China Press. 2005.

129. Shi Feng. Fundamentals of information theory [M]. Wuhan University Press.2014

130. Anduiza, E., Cristancho, C. & Sabucedo, J. (2011) 'The political protest of the out- raged in Spain: what's new?'. Unpublished manuscript, used with permission.

131. Bauman, Z. (2000) Liquid Modernity, Polity, Cambridge. Beck, U. & Beck-Gersheim, E. (2002) Individualization: Institutionalized Individual.

132. Ism and its Social and Political Consequences, SAGE, London. Benford, R. D. & Snow, D. A. (2000) 'Framing processes and social movements: an overview and an assessment', Annual Review of Sociology, vol. 26, pp. 611–639.

133. Benkler, Y. (2006) The Wealth of Networks: How Social Production Transforms Markets and Freedom, Yale University Press, New Haven.

134. Bennett, W. L. (1998) 'The uncivic culture: communication, identity, and the rise of lifestyle politics', Ithiel de Sola Pool Lecture, American Political Science Association, published in P.S.: Political Science and Politics, vol. 31 (December), pp. 41–61.

135. Bennett, W. L. (2003) 'Communicating global activism: strengths and vulnerabilities of networked politics', Information, Communication & Society, vol. 6, no. 2, pp. 143–168.

136. Bennett, W. L. (2005) 'Social movements beyond borders: organization, communi- cation, and political capacity in two eras of transnational activism', in Transna- tional Protest and Global Activism, eds D. della Porta & S. Tarrow, Rowman & Littlefield, Boulder, CO, pp. 203–226.

137. Bennett, W. L. & Segerberg, A. (2011) 'Digital media and the personalization of collec- tive action: social technology and

the organization of protests against the global economic crisis', Information, Communication & Society, vol. 14, pp. 770–799.

138. Bimber, B. & Davis, R. (2003) Campaigning Online: The Internet in U.S. Elections, Oxford University Press, New York.

139. Bimber, B., Stohl, C. & Flanagin, A. (2009) 'Technological change and the shifting nature of political organization', in Routledge Handbook of Internet Politics, eds A. Chadwick & P. Howard, Routledge, London, pp. 72–85.

140. Bimber, B., Flanagin, A. & Stohl, C. (in press) Collective Action in Organizations: Inter- action and Engagement and Engagement in an Era of Technological Change, Cam- bridge University Press, New York.

141. Calderaro, A. (2011) 'New political struggles in the network society: the case of free and open source software (FOSS) Movement', paper presented at ECPR General Conference, Reykjavik, 25–27 August 2011.

142. Castells, M. (2000) The Network Society, 2nd edn, Blackwell, Oxford.Chadwick, A. (2007) 'Digital network repertoires and organizational hybridity', Pol-

143. Conference, Reykjavik, Iceland, 25–27 August 2011.Chesters, G. & Welsh, I. (2006) Complexity and Social Movements: Multitudes at the End of Chaos, Routledge, London.

144. Dawkins, R. (1989) The Selfish Gene, Oxford University Press, Oxford.Diani, M. (2011) The Cement of Civil Society: Civic Networks in Local Settings, Barcelona, unpublished manuscript.

145. Hunt, S., Benford, R. D. & Snow, D. A. (1994) 'Identity fields: framing processes and the social construction of movement identities', in New Social Movements: From Ideology to Identity, eds E. Laraña, H. Johnston & J. R. Gusfield, Temple University Press, Philadelphia, pp. 185–208.

146. Inglehart, R. (1997) Modernization and Post-Modernization: Cultural, Economic and Pol- itical Change in 43 Societies, Princeton University Press, Princeton.

147. Juris, J. (2008) Networking Futures: The Movements against Corporate Globalization, Duke University Press, Durham, NC.

148. Keck, M. & Sikkink, K. (1998) Activists Beyond Borders: Advocacy Networks in Inter- national Politics, Cornell University Press, Ithaca, NY.

149. Latour, B. (2005) Reassembling the Social: An Introduction to Actor-Network-Theory, Oxford University Press, Oxford.

150. Livingston, S. & Asmolov, G. (2010) 'Networks and the future of foreign affairs reporting', Journalism Studies, vol. 11, no. 5, pp. 745–760.

151. Lupia, A. & Sin, G. (2003) 'Which public goods are endangered? How evolving communication technologies affect "The Logic of Collective Action"', Public Choice, vol. 117, pp. 315–331.

152. McAdam, D. (1986) 'Recruitment to high-risk activism: The case of freedom summer', American Journal of Sociology, vol. 92, pp. 64–90.

153. McAdam, D., McCarthy, J. D. & Zald, M. N. (eds) (1996) 'Introduction: opportu- nities, mobilizing structures, and framing processes – toward a synthetic, comparative perspective on social movements', in Comparative Perspectives on Social Movements: Political Opportunities, Mobilizing Structures, and Cultural Framings, Cambridge University Press, New York.

154. McAdam, D., Tarrow, S. & Tilly, C. (2001) Dynamics of Contention, Cambridge University Press, New York.

155. McCarthy, J. D. & Zald, M. N. (1973) The Trend of Social Movements in America: Profes- sionalization and Resource Mobilization, General Learning Press, Morristown, NJ. McCarthy.

156. J. D. & Zald, M. N. (1977) 'Resource mobilization and social move- ments: a partial theory', American Journal of Sociology, vol. 82, no. 6, pp. 1212–1241.

157. McDonald, K. (2002) 'From solidarity to fluidarity: social movements beyond "collective identity" – the case of globalization conflicts', Social Movement Studies, vol. 1, no. 2, pp. 109–128.

158. Melucci, A. (1996) Challenging Codes: Collective Action in the Information Age, Cam- bridge University Press, Cambridge.

159. Micheletti, M. (2003) Political Virtue and Shopping, Palgrave, New York.Morozov, E. (2011) The Net Delusion: How Not to Liberate the World, Allen Lane, London.

160. Olson, M. (1965) The Logic of Collective Action: Public Goods and the Theory of Groups, Harvard University Press, Cambridge.

161. MA.Polletta, F. (2002) Freedom Is an Endless meeting. Democracy in American Social Move- ments, University of Chicago Press, Chicago.

162. Porta, D. (2005) 'Multiple belongings, flexible identities and the construction of "another politics": between the European social forum and the local social fora', in Transnational Protest and Global Activism,

163. Rheingold, H. (2002) Smart Mobs: The Next Social Revolution, Perseus Pub., Cambridge, MA.

164. Robinson, A. & Tormey, S. (2005) 'Horizontals, Verticals and the Conflicting Logics of Transformative Politics', in Confronting Globalization, eds C. el-Ojeili & P. Hayden, Palgrave, London, pp. 208–226.

165. Routledge, P. & Cumbers, A. (2009) Global Justice Networks: Geographies of Transna- tional Solidarity, Manchester University Press, Manchester, UK.

166. Segerberg, A. & Bennett, W. L. (2011) 'Social media and the organization of collective action: using Twitter to explore the ecologies of two climate change protests', The Communication Review, vol. 14, no. 3, pp. 197–215.

167. Snow, D. A., Rochford, B.Jr., Worden, S. K. & Benford, R. D. (1986) 'Frame align- ment processes, micromobilization, and movement participation', American Sociological Review, vol. 51, pp. 464–481.

168. Tarrow, S. (2011) Power in Movement: Social Movements in Contentious Politics, 3rd edn, Cambridge University Press, New York.

169. Tilly, C. (2004) Social Movements, 1768–2004, Paradigm, Boulder, CO.Tilly, C. (2006) 'WUNC', in Crowds, eds J. T. Schnapp & M. Tiews, Stanford University Press, Stanford, pp. 289–306.

170. Acquisti, A. & Gross, R. (2009) 'Predicting social security numbers from public data', Proceedings of the National Academy of Science, vol. 106, no. 27, pp. 10975–10980.

171. Baca, G. (2004) 'Legends of Fordism: between myth, history, and foregone con- clusions', Social Analysis, vol. 48, no. 3, pp. 169–178.

172. Behar, R. & Gordon, D. A. (eds) (1996) Women Writing Culture, University of Cali- fornia Press, Berkeley, CA.

173. Berry, D. (2011) 'The computational turn: thinking about the digital humanities', Culture Machine, vol. 12, [Online] Available at: http://www. culturemachine.net/index.php/cm/article/view/440/470 (11 July 2011).

174. Blass, T. (2004) The Man Who Shocked the World: The Life and Legacy of Stanley Milgram, Basic Books, New York.

175. San Francisco, and Oxford.Cain, M. & Finch, J. (1981) 'Towards a rehabilitation of data', in Practice and Progress: British Sociology 1950–1980, eds P. Abrams, R. Deem, J. Finch & P. Rock,

176. George Allen and Unwin, London, pp. 105–119.Clifford, J. & Marcus, G. E. (eds) (1986) Writing Culture: The Poetics and Politics of Ethnography, University of California Press, Berkeley, CA.

177. Crawford, K. (2009) 'Following you: disciplines of listening in social media', Con- tinuum: Journal of Media & Cultural Studies, vol. 23, no. 4, pp. 532–533.

178. Derrida, J. (1996) Archive Fever: A Freudian Impression, trans. Eric Prenowitz, Univer- sity of Chicago Press, Chicago.

179. Dourish, P. & Bell, G. (2011) Divining a Digital Future: Mess and Mythology in Ubiqui- tous Computing, MIT Press, Cambridge, MA.

180. Du Gay, P. & Pryke, M. (2002) Cultural Economy: Cultural Analysis and Commercial Life, Sage, London.

181. Durkheim, E. (1895/1982) Rules of Sociological Method, The Free Press, New York, NY.

182. Fischer, C. (1982) To Dwell Among Friends: Personal Networks in Town and City, University of Chicago, Chicago.

183. Forsythe, D. (2001) Studying Those Who Study Us: An Anthropologist in the World of Arti- ficial Intelligence, Stanford University Press, Stanford.

184. Freeman, L. (2006) The Development of Social Network Analysis, Empirical Press, Vancouver.

185. Fry, J. P. & Sibley, E. H. (1996) [1974] 'Evolution of database management systems', Computing Surveys, vol. 8, no. 1.1, pp. 7–42. Reprinted in (1996) Great Papers in Computer Science, ed. L. Laplante, IEEE Press, New York.

186. Granovetter, M. S. (1973) 'The strength of weak ties', American Journal of Sociology, vol. 78, no. 6, pp. 1360–1380.

187. Harding, S. (2010) 'Feminism, science and the anti-Enlightenment critiques', in Women, Knowledge and Reality: Explorations in Feminist Philosophy, eds A. Garry & M. Pearsall, Unwin Hyman, Boston, MA, pp. 298–320.

188. Homans, G. C. (1974) Social Behavior: Its Elementary Forms, Harvard University Press, Cambridge, MA.

189. Kranzberg, M. (1986) 'Technology and history: kranzberg's laws', Technology and Culture, vol. 27, no. 3, pp. 544–560.

190. Latour, B. (2009) 'Tarde's idea of quantification', in The Social after Gabriel Tarde: Debates and Assessments, ed. M. Candea, Routledge, London, pp. 145–162,

191. N., Contractor, N., Fowler, J., Gutmann, M., Jebara, T., King, G., Macy, M., Roy, D. & Van Alstyne, M. (2009) 'Computational social science', Science, vol. 323, no. 5915, pp. 721–723.

192. Leinweber, D. (2007) 'Stupid data miner tricks: overfitting the S&P 500', The Journal of Investing, vol. 16, no. 1, pp. 15–22.

193. Lessig, L. (1999) Code: and Other Laws of Cyberspace, Basic Books, New York, NY.

194. Lewis, K., Kaufman, J., Gonzalez, M., Wimmer, A. & Christakis, N. (2008) 'Tastes, ties, and time: a new social network dataset using Facebook.com',Social Networks, vol. 30, no. 4, pp. 330–342.

195. Fidler,Roger. (1997)Mediamorphosis: Understanding the New Media.

196. Clement H. C. Leung,Alice W. S. Chan,Alfredo Milani,Jiming Liu,Yuanxi Li. ACM Transactions on Intelligent Systems and Technology (TIST) . (2012)Intelligent Social Media Indexing and Sharing Using an Adaptive Indexing Search Engine[J] .

197. Christy M.K. Cheung,Pui-Yee Chiu,Matthew K.O. Lee. Computers in Human Behavior . (2010)Online social networks: Why do students use facebook?[J] .

198. Boyd-Barrett, Oliver. Global Media andCommunication. (2006)"Cyberspace, Globalization and Empire.".

199. Natalya N. Bazarova,Yoon Hyung Choi. J Commun . (2014)Self-Disclosure in Social Media: Extending the Functional Approach to Disclosure Motivations and Characteristics on Social Network Sites[An earlier][J] .

200. Soroush Vosoughi,Deb Roy,Sinan Aral. Science. (2018)The spread of true and false news online[J] .

201. Lawson-Borders,G. The International Journal on Media Management . (2003)'Integrating New Media and Old Media:Seven Observations of Convergence as a Strategy for Best Practices in Media Organizations'.

202. Zongyang Ma,Aixin Sun,Gao Cong. J Am Soc Inf Sci Tec . (2013)On predicting the popularity of newly emerging hashtags in Twitter[J] .

203. Erkan,Evans. Journal of Marketing Communications . (2018) Social media or shopping websites? The influence of eWOM on consumers' online purchase intentions[J] .

204. Thomas F,Baldwin, D,Stevens McVoy,Charles Steinfield. (1996)Convergence: Integrating media, Information & Communication.

205. Stuart Palmer. International Journal of Virtual Communities and . (2015)Tracking Comet ISON through the Twittersphere: Visualizing Science Communication in Social Media[J] .

206. Borae Jin. Computers in Human Behavior. (2013)How lonely people use and perceive Facebook[J].

207. Jenkins,Henry. Convergence Culture: Where Old and New MediCollide . (2006)"Introduction: Worship at the Altar of

Convergence: A NewParadigm for Understanding Media Chang.".

208. Yang,Lin,Carlson,Ross. Journal of Marketing Management . (2016)Brand engagement on social media: will firms' social media efforts influence search engine advertising effectiveness?[J] .

209. Ravi S. Sharma,Margaret Tan,Francis Pereira. Business Science Reference . (2012) Understanding the Interactive Digital Media Marketplace:Frameworks, Platforms, Communities and Issues.

210. Tracii Ryan,Sophia Xenos. Computers in Human Behavior . (2011)Who uses Facebook? An investigation into the relationship between the Big Five, shyness, narcissism, loneliness, and Facebook usage[J] .

211. Geoffrey G. Parker,Marshall W. Van Alstyne. Management Science .(2005)Two-Sided Network Effects: A Theory of Information Product Design[J] .

212. Krug,S. (2005)Don"t Make Me Think!: A Common Sense Approach to Web Usability.

213. Shin,Dong-Hee. info . (2006)"Convergence of telecommunications, media and information technology, and implications for regulation".

214. Mohammad Valipour,Mohammad Ebrahim Banihabib,Seyyed Mahmood Reza Behbahani. Journal of Hydrology .(2013) Comparison of the ARMA, ARIMA, and the autoregressive artificial neural network models in forecasting the monthly inflow of Dez dam reservoir[J] .

215. I.F. Akyildiz,W. Su,Y. Sankarasubramaniam,E. Cayirci. Computer Networks . (2002)Wireless sensor networks: a survey[J] .

216. Fu-Guo Deng,Bao-Cang Ren,Xi-Han Li. Science Bulletin . (2017) Quantum hyperentanglement and its applications in quantum information processing[J] .

217. Dong, Ruifang,Lassen, Mikael,Heersink, Joel,Marquardt, Christoph,Filip, Radim,Leuchs, Gerd,Andersen, Ulrik L. Nature Physics . (2008)Experimental entanglement distillation of mesoscopic quantum states[J] .

218. Guo-Feng Zhang,Heng Fan,Ai-Ling Ji,Zhao-Tan Jiang,Ahmad Abliz,Wu-Ming Liu. Annals of Physics . (2011)Quantum correlations in spin models[J] .

219. Lanyon, Benjamin P,Barbieri, Marco,Almeida, Marcelo P,Jennewein, Thomas,Ralph, Timothy C,Resch, Kevin J,Pryde, Geoff J,O'brien, Jeremy L,Gilchrist, Alexei,White, Andrew G. Nature Physics . (2009)Simplifying quantum logic using higher-dimensional Hilbert spaces[J] .

220. Jaehyun Park,Sung H. Han,Hyun K. Kim,Seunghwan Oh,Heekyung Moon. International Journal of Industrial Ergonomics .(2013)Modeling user experience: A case study on a mobile device[J].

Printed in the United States
by Baker & Taylor Publisher Services